FOUNDATIONS

Second Edition

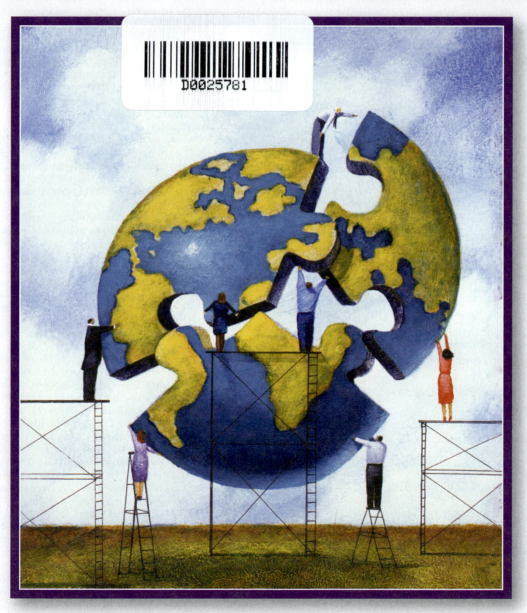

D0025781

Steven J. Molinsky • Bill Bliss

PEARSON
Longman

Foundations, second edition

Copyright © 2007 by Prentice Hall Regents
Pearson Education, Inc.
All rights reserved.

No part of this publication may be reproduced, stored in a retrieval system, or transmitted in any form or by any means, electronic, mechanical, photocopying, recording, or otherwise, without the prior permission of the publisher.

Pearson Education, 10 Bank Street, White Plains, NY 10606

Editorial director: Pam Fishman
Vice president, director of design and production: Rhea Banker
Director of electronic production: Aliza Greenblatt
Director of manufacturing: Patrice Fraccio
Senior manufacturing manager: Edith Pullman
Director of marketing: Oliva Fernandez
Production editor: Diane Cipollone; Christine Cervoni,
    Camelot Editorial Services, LLC
Text composition: Word & Image Design Studio, Inc.
Text design: Wanda España, Wee Design Group; Warren
    Fischbach; Wendy Wolf
Cover design: Wanda España, Wee Design Group; Warren
    Fischbach; Wendy Wolf
Art management: Diane Cipollone, Paula Williams
Realia creation: Paul McCusker, Word & Image Design
Contributing artist: François Escamel
Contributing photographers: David Mager, Elbaliz Mendez,
    Pearson Learning Group Photo Studio
Director, Image Resource Center: Melinda Reo
Manager, Rights and Permissions: Zina Arabia
Manager, Visual Research: Beth Brenzel
Manager, Cover Visual Research & Permissions: Karen
    Sanatar
Image permission coordinator: Angelique Sharps
Photo researcher: Terri Stratford

Principal photographer: Paul I. Tañedo
Illustrations: Richard E. Hill

Library of Congress Cataloging-in-Publication Data

Molinsky, Steven J.
    Foundations / Steven J. Molinsky, Bill Bliss.—2nd ed.
        p. cm.
    Includes index.
    ISBN 978-0-13-173144-8 / 0-13-173144-0
    1. English language—Textbooks for foreign speakers. I.
Bliss, Bill. II. Title.
PE1128.M676 2007
428.3'4—dc22   2005044357

Longman on the Web
Longman.com offers online resources for teachers and students.

Access our Companion Websites, our online catalog, and our local offices around the world.

Visit us at longman.com.

Printed in the United States of America
18 19 20 21 22 —V082—17 16 15

Additional photos: pp.2–3 (header) Digital Vision/Getty Images, Inc.; p.15 (top, far left) Corbis Royalty Free; (top, 2nd from left) Robert Brenner/PhotoEdit Inc.; (top, 2nd from right) Peter Byron/PhotoEdit Inc.; (top, far right) Christine Schneider/Zefa/Corbis-Zefa Collection; pp.18–19 (header) Barry Rosenthal/Getty Images, Inc./Taxi; p.29 (top, left) Andrew Gunner/Getty Images, Inc./Digital Vision; (top, right) Joanna B. Pinneo/Aurora/Getty Images, Inc.; p.32 (header, top left) Getty Images, Inc./Image Source; (header, 2nd image from left) Getty Images, Inc./Photodisc; (header, far right) EyeWire Collection/Getty Images, Inc./Photodisc; p.33 (header, top right) Getty Images, Inc./Photodisc; p.40 (middle row, left) Shoichi Itoga/Getty Images, Inc.; (middle row, right) L. Roger Turner/Corbis/Sygma; (bottom row, left) TAMARA VONINSKI/Photolibrary.com; (bottom row, center) Zanna/Fotolia; (bottom row, right) Magalhaes, Paulo/Getty Images, Inc./Image Bank; p.41 (top row, 1st) Magalhaes, Paulo/Getty Images, Inc./Image Bank; (top row, 2nd) Shoichi Itoga/Getty Images, Inc.; (top row, 3rd) L. Roger Turner/Corbis/Sygma; (top row, 4th) Zanna/Fotolia; p.46–47 (header) Getty Images, Inc./Photodisc; p.64–65 (header) Rob Melnychuk/Getty Images, Inc./Photodisc; p.65 (top row, 2nd) Diane Cipollone; p.71 (middle row, right) Myrleen Ferguson Cate/PhotoEdit, Inc.; (bottom row, left) Speedfighter/Fotolia; (bottom row, center) Rene Sheret/Getty Images, Inc./Stone Allstock; (bottom row, right) Bob Rowan/Corbis/Bettmann; p.73 (top row, 1st) Bruno Morandi/Robert Harding/Getty Images, Inc.; (top row, 2nd) Robert van der Hilst/CORBIS-NY/© Robert van der Hilst/CORBIS All Rights Reserved; (top row, 3rd) Kevin R. Morris/CORBIS-NY/© Kevin R. Morris/CORBIS All Rights Reserved; (top row, 4th) Dave G. Houser/Post-Houserstock/CORBIS-NY/© Dave G. Houser/CORBIS All Rights Reserved; pp.76–77 (header) F. Castagna; p.77 (top row, right) Corbis Premium RF/Alamy; p.80 (bottom row, 2nd) Corbis Premium RF/Alamy; p.81 (top, 4th) Corbis Premium RF/Alamy; p.85 (top row, 4th) imagebroker/Alamy; p.88–89 (header) Chuck Savage/Corbis/Bettmann; p.96 (2nd row, left) Cardinale Stephane/Corbis/Sygma; (2nd row, center) Peter Turnley/CORBIS-NY/© Peter Turnley/CORBIS All Rights Reserved; (2nd row, right) Owen Franken/CORBIS-NY/© Owen Franken/CORBIS All Rights Reserved; (3rd row, left) Corbis Royalty Free; (3rd row, center) Corbis Royalty Free; (3rd row, right) Corbis Royalty Free; (bottom row, left) Robert Stelzer/SambaPhoto/Getty Images, Inc./SambaPhoto; (bottom row, center) Jim Whitmer/Jim Whitmer Photography; (bottom row, right) Sandro Vannini/CORBIS-NY/© Sandro Vannini/CORBIS All Rights Reserved; p.102–103 (header) Getty Images, Inc./Stockbyte; p.118–119 (header) Punchstock/Image Source/Punchstock; p.129 (top row, left) Stockbyte; (top row, center) Kerstin Geier/CORBIS-NY/© Kerstin Geier/CORBIS All Rights Reserved; (top row, right) ZUMA Wire Service/Alamy; p.132 (header, left) Getty Images, Inc./Digital Vision; (header, right) Adam Gault/Digital Vision/Getty Images, Inc.; p.133 (header) Getty Images, Inc./Image Source; p.144–145 (header) PhotoLink/Photodisc Green/Getty Images, Inc./Photodisc; p.144 (left) Corbis Royalty Free; (right) Corbis Royalty Free; p.158–159 EyeWire Collection/Getty Images, Inc./Photodisc; p.167 (top row, left) AP Wide World Photos; (top row, center) Michael S. Lewis/CORBIS-NY/© Michael S. Lewis/CORBIS All Rights Reserved; (top row, right) James Marshall/CORBIS-NY/© James Marshall/CORBIS All Rights Reserved; p.170–171 (header) C. Sherburne/Getty Images, Inc./Photodisc; p.170 (#2) Corbis Royalty Free; (bottom row, left) Robert Ginn/Unicorn Stock Photos; p.185 (top row, 1st) AP Wide World Photos; (top row, 2nd) Dean Conger/CORBIS-NY/© Dean Conger/CORBIS All Rights Reserved; (top row, 3rd) Peter Turnley/CORBIS-NY/© Peter Turnley/CORBIS All Rights Reserved; (top row, 4th) Macduff Everton/CORBIS-NY/©Macduff Everton/CORBIS All rights Reserved; p.188–189 (header) Chris Hondros/Reportage/Getty Images, Inc.; p.188 (2nd) Diane Cipollone; (7th) F. Castagna; p.194 (top, left) Getty Images/Photodisc/Ryan McVay; p.199 (top row, left) Michael T. Sedam/CORBIS-NY/© Michael T. Sedam/CORBIS All Rights Reserved; (top row, right) mgrushin/Fotolia; (2nd row, left) Jose Canas/©Jose Canas; (2nd row, right) Image Source/Getty Images; p.202 (header, top left) Chris Leslie Smith/PhotoEdit, Inc.; (header, top right) Terry Wild/The Terry Wild Studio, Inc.; p.203 (bottom row, left) Corbis Premium RF/Alamy; p.207 (top row, center) Corbis Premium RF/Alamy; p.211 (top row, 1st) Corbis Royalty Free; (top row, 3rd) Jess Stock/Getty Images, Inc./Stone Allstock; (top row, 3rd) Jose Carrillo/PhotoEdit, Inc.; (top row, 4th) Jon Burbank/The Image Works

Cover photos: (top) Jeffrey, David/Getty Images, Inc./Image Bank; (top, right) Adam Gault/Digital Vision/Getty Images, Inc.; (center, right) Getty Images, Inc./Stockbyte; (bottom, right) Punchstock/Image Source; (right) Dave Cutler/CORBIS Images.com

Contents

Guide to Unit and Lesson Features

Foundations is an all-skills, standards-based program for beginning-literacy and low-beginning learners of English. Its clear and easy-to-use format offers students an introduction to basic English for essential lifeskill situations and builds a language *foundation* for students' future success at the Book 1 level of instruction.

Competency-based units in a careful, research-based sequence integrate students' development of language skills with lifeskill topics that begin with the immediate world of the student and then progress to the world at large.

Standards-based instruction helps students develop key competencies included in CASAS, BEST Plus, EFF, SCANS, Model Standards, and other major state and local curriculum frameworks and assessment systems.

Unit 2 — The Classroom

Goals
▶ Classroom objects
▶ Classroom actions
▶ Numbers 11 – 19

Vocabulary Preview

1 board	5 calculator	9 computer
2 book	6 chair	10 desk
3 bookshelf	7 chalk	11 eraser
4 bulletin board	8 clock	12 globe

1 map	5 pencil	9 table
2 notebook	6 ruler	10 teacher
3 overhead projector	7 screen	11 TV
4 pen	8 student	12 wall

18   19

Photo dictionary pages at the beginning of each unit offer learners a clear visual reference for mastering key vocabulary.

Essential lifeskills vocabulary is introduced through context-rich photos and easy-to-use word lists. Students practice more than 350 key words in these vocabulary preview lessons—especially helpful preparation for the low-beginning learner.

Convenient two-page lessons follow an easy-to-use format that is consistent and predictable—specifically designed for students with limited prior experience using a textbook.

Simple, accessible dialogs introduce lesson objectives through authentic communicative contexts.

Highlighted words in color and **"skeletal dialogs"** with blanks help students focus on key vocabulary and practice new conversations.

All-skills activities provide ample practice in listening, reading, writing, vocabulary, and basic grammar.

Real-life conversation practice gets students talking from the first moments of each new lesson through active pair work that maximizes student participation.

Extensive photos and illustrations provide contexts and support vocabulary learning.

Action-oriented instruction includes movement activities and games to create a lively, participatory classroom for low-beginning students with a range of learning styles.

Community tasks introduce basic civics topics related to community life and help students connect to community services.

Numbers lessons in every unit provide a careful introduction to basic numeracy and math skills—fully-coordinated with the communicative, vocabulary, and topic objectives of the unit.

Simple journal-writing opportunities encourage students to write basic sentences to apply the unit's vocabulary and topics to their own lives and then share their writing with other students—a gentle introduction to writing for the low-beginning student.

Photos from around the world provide a springboard for student sharing and cross-cultural discussions about how people's lives are different in other countries and cultures.

Information gap activities in every unit promote teamwork and communication practice as pairs of students work together to complete tasks by sharing information and cooperating.

Cooperative learning tasks in information gap activities include completing simple inventories and schedules, filling out forms, and reading maps.

Vocabulary lists and language skill checklists help students review words they have learned and keep track of the skills they are developing.

Full-page illustrations stimulate a range of activities for individual students, pairs, small groups, and the entire class. Activities include: vocabulary review; identifying characters, actions, and contexts; predicting situations and what people are saying; practicing conversations; expansion activities and games.

Color overhead transparencies of these illustrations promote active full-class vocabulary practice and lively class participation during illustration-based activities and games.

Scope and Sequence

LANGUAGE SKILLS & STANDARDS-BASED OBJECTIVES

UNIT	KEY TOPICS	LISTENING & SPEAKING	READING & WRITING	NUMERACY/ MATH
1 **Personal Information & Family** *Page 2*	• The alphabet • Numbers 0–10 • Introduce yourself • Spell your name • Telephone numbers • Addresses • Family members	• Greeting people • Introducing yourself • Spelling name aloud • Listening to names spelled aloud & choosing correct written form • Asking & answering questions about name & spelling, address, & telephone number • Repeating information to check understanding • Listening to phone numbers & apartment numbers & choosing correct written form • Introducing family members • Talking about a family photo	• Identifying & writing alphabet letters • Reading information on a form • Filling out a form with personal information (name, address, telephone, cell phone, e-mail) • Writing telephone numbers • Identifying abbreviations for states • Interpreting a family tree diagram • Writing about family members	• Numbers 0–10 • Telephone numbers • Numbers in addresses (street numbers, apartment numbers, zip codes) • Using numbers to indicate age • Social security numbers
2 **The Classroom** *Page 18*	• Classroom objects • Classroom actions • Numbers 11–19	• Identifying classroom objects & locations • Locating classroom objects • Identifying classroom actions • Giving & following simple classroom commands • Listening to & identifying classroom objects & actions • Describing objects & people's actions in a classroom scene	• Making a list of objects • Reading an inventory list of objects • Writing a description of a classroom	• Numbers 11–19 • Using numbers to indicate quantity • Using numbers to take inventory
3 **Everyday Activities & Weather** *Page 32*	• Describe everyday activities • Numbers 20–100 • Describe weather • Interpret a weather map	• Talking about everyday activities • Inquiring by phone about a person's activities • Listening to & identifying everyday activities • Describing the weather • Listening to & identifying weather descriptions • Asking & answering personal information questions	• Arranging a list of events into chronological order • Interpreting a weather map • Reading weather information in a newspaper • Making a list of cities & weather conditions • Writing about daily activities	• Numbers 20–100 • Temperatures • Using numbers to indicate age • Using numbers to indicate address
4 **Numbers, Time, Calendar, Money** *Page 46*	• Cardinal numbers 1–100 • Time • Days of the week • Ordinal numbers • Months of the year • Coins & currency	• Asking & answering addition problems • Listening & identifying numbers, times • Asking & telling time • Saying days of the week & months of the year • Making an appointment over the telephone • Asking & answering about where you live • Saying a date • Asking & giving information about birthday • Listening & identifying dates • Saying names & values of coins & currency • Listening & identifying amounts of money • Asking & giving information about a transportation schedule	• Reading addition problems • Writing numbers • Reading clock times • Recognizing abbreviations of days of the week & months of the year • Writing days of the week & months of the year • Writing time information on a calendar • Writing dates of birthdays & holidays • Writing about daily schedule	• Cardinal numbers 1–100 • Ordinal numbers • Addition • Pronouncing numbers • Listening & identifying similar numbers • Saying large address numbers & room numbers • Telling time • Identifying times on schedules • Using ordinal numbers to indicate order, dates, birthdays • Coin & currency values • Adding coin & currency values

CURRICULUM STANDARDS & FRAMEWORKS

BASIC GRAMMAR*	COMMUNITY/ CIVICS & CULTURE	EFF	SCANS	CASAS	LAUSD	FLORIDA Foundations	FLORIDA Low Beginning
• WH-Questions: *Who, What, How* • Personal pronouns: *I, you, he, she* • Possessive adjectives: *my, his, her*	• Emergency telephone numbers: Police, Ambulance, Fire, Poison control center • Greeting people in different cultures	• Interact in a way that is friendly • Identify community resources • Identify family relationships • Respect others & value diversity • Cooperate with others • Work together	• Sociability • Acquire information • Communicate information • Work with cultural diversity	0.1.2, 0.1.4, 0.2.1, 0.2.2	*Beg. Literacy:* 1, 2, 3, 4, 5 *Beg. Low:* 1, 2, 4, 6, 7, 9, 58	5.01, 5.02, 6.04, 8.01, 10.02, 12.01, 14.01, 15.02, 15.03, 15.04, 15.05, 15.06, 15.07, 16.01, 16.02, 16.04, 16.05, 16.06, 16.10, 16.11	5.01, 5.02, 6.04, 10.02, 14.01, 15.02, 15.05, 15.06, 15.07, 16.01, 16.02, 16.04, 16.05, 16.06, 16.10, 16.11
• Verb: To be • Yes/No questions • WH-Questions: *What, Where, How many* • Prepositions of location: *on, next to* • Articles: *a, an* • There is / There are • Imperatives	• Visiting a classroom in another school • Comparing classrooms in different countries	• Manage resources: Identify those resources you have; Determine where they are • Give direction • Respect others & value diversity • Cooperate with others • Work together	• Basic skills • Identify resources • Work with cultural diversity • Participate as a member of a team	0.1.2, 0.1.5	*Beg. Literacy:* 8, 9, 11 *Beg. Low:* 12, 13, 15, 16, 17, 18	5.01, 8.01, 15.03, 15.04, 15.06, 15.07, 16.02, 16.04, 16.05, 16.06, 16.08, 16.09, 16.10, 16.11	5.01, 8.01, 15.02, 15.06, 15.07, 16.02, 16.04, 16.05, 16.06, 16.08, 16.09, 16.10, 16.11
• Simple present tense • Present continuous tense • WH-Questions: *What, How old*	• Using newspaper weather maps & weather reports • How household chores are shared in different cultures	• Meet family needs & responsibilities • Organize activities • Identify family relationships • Gather information • Understand & interpret numbers • Respect others & value diversity • Cooperate with others • Work together	• Basic skills • Identify goal-relevant activities • Work with cultural diversity • Participate as a member of a team	0.1.2, 0.1.4, 0.2.1, 0.2.4, 1.1.5, 2.1.8, 2.3.3, 7.5.5, 7.5.6, 8.2.3	*Beg. Literacy:* 5, 6 *Beg. Low:* 9, 11, 12, 13, 28, 29	5.01, 5.02, 8.01, 13.01, 14.01, 15.03, 15.04, 15.06, 15.07, 16.01, 16.02, 16.05, 16.06, 16.07, 16.09, 16.11	5.01, 5.02, 7.08, 13.01, 14.01, 15.02, 15.06, 15.07, 16.01, 16.02, 16.05, 16.06, 16.07, 16.09, 16.11
• WH-Questions: *How much, What* • Can	• Making appointments • Writing days & times of work & school schedules • Using a transportation schedule • Concepts of time & punctuality in different cultures	• Acquire information • Understand, interpret, & work with numbers • Use math to solve problems • Manage resources: Allocate time • Respect others & value diversity • Cooperate with others • Work together	• Basic skills • Acquire & communicate information • Sociability: Demonstrate friendliness • Self-management • Work with cultural diversity • Participate as a member of a team	0.1.2, 0.2.1, 1.1.6, 2.3.1, 2.3.2, 6.1.1	*Beg. Literacy:* 6, 12, 13 *Beg. Low:* 3, 4, 25, 26, 30	5.01, 5.02, 8.01, 8.02, 8.03, 8.05, 11.01, 15.03, 15.04, 15.06, 15.07, 16.01, 16.02, 16.05, 16.06, 16.08, 16.10, 16.11	5.01, 5.02, 8.01, 8.02, 8.03, 8.04, 15.02, 15.06, 15.07, 16.01, 16.02, 16.05, 16.06, 16.08, 16.10, 16.11

* Basic grammar structures are included in a careful progression for introductory exposure, not mastery.

EFF: Equipped for the Future (Content standards, Common activities, & Key activities for Citizen/Community Member, Worker, & Parent/Family role maps; EFF communication skills are covered in every unit)

SCANS: Secretary's Commission on Achieving Necessary Skills (U.S. Department of Labor)

CASAS: Comprehensive Adult Student Assessment System

LAUSD: Los Angeles Unified School District content standards (Beginning Literacy, Beginning Low)

FLORIDA: Adult ESOL Standardized Syllabi

(‡Florida benchmarks 17.01, 17.02, and 17.03 are covered in every unit and therefore are not included in the listings above.)

Scope and Sequence

LANGUAGE SKILLS & STANDARDS-BASED OBJECTIVES

UNIT	KEY TOPICS	LISTENING & SPEAKING	READING & WRITING	NUMERACY/ MATH
5 **Home** *Page 64*	• Rooms in the home • Home appliances & features • Types of housing	• Identifying rooms in the home • Identifying home appliances & features • Asking for information about an apartment • Asking & answering questions about home activities • Identifying furniture • Asking for & giving instructions • Talking about types of housing in the community	• Understanding number information in a story • Writing a description of your home	• Cardinal & ordinal numbers review • Understanding number information in a story
6 **Community** *Page 76*	• Places in the community • Asking for & giving location	• Identifying places in the community • Asking & answering questions about destination • Listening & identifying places in the community • Asking & giving the location of places in the community • Getting someone's attention politely	• Reading & writing missing words in a cloze paragraph about people's activities • Writing missing letters in words • Reading street names • Writing addresses of community services • Writing about your neighborhood • Interpreting a simple street map	• Ordinal numbers in names of streets
7 **Describing** *Page 88*	• Describing people: Age, Height, Hair color, Eye color, Marital status • Describing feelings • Countries & languages • Titles	• Describing people by physical characteristics • Asking & answering questions about age, height, hair color, eye color, weight • Making a request at work • Asking & telling what someone looks like • Listening & identifying a person by a physical description • Asking & giving personal information: marital status, country of origin, language spoken • Inquiring about & describing feelings	• Reading & writing missing words in a cloze paragraph about family members' activities • Completing a chart about family members • Completing a chart with descriptive information about people • Making a list of students, their countries, & their languages • Filling out a personal information form • Writing about yourself	• Using numbers to indicate age, height, weight
8 **Food** *Page 102*	• Common foods • Expressing food needs • Food containers & quantities • Ordering food in a restaurant	• Identifying food items • Expressing food needs • Listening & identifying food items • Locating food items in a store • Identifying food containers & quantities • Ordering food items in a fast-food restaurant or coffee shop • Taking customers' orders at a food service counter • Identifying units of measure • Making a polite request	• Categorizing: Listing words in correct groups • Writing missing letters in words • Making a list of food stores & foods purchased there • Making a list of fast-food restaurants & foods eaten there • Interpreting abbreviations for food measurements (lb., qt., doz.) • Making a food shopping list • Writing about favorite food	• Aisle numbers in stores • Food quantities (quart, pound, half a pound, dozen, half a dozen)

CURRICULUM STANDARDS & FRAMEWORKS

BASIC GRAMMAR	COMMUNITY/ CIVICS & CULTURE	EFF	SCANS	CASAS	LAUSD	FLORIDA	
						FOUNDATIONS	LOW BEGINNING
• Has • There is / There are • WH-Questions: *How many, Where* • Imperatives	• Types of housing in a community • Comparing different kinds of homes around the world	• Give direction • Meet family needs • Identify community resources • Respect others & value diversity • Cooperate with others • Work together	• Basic skills • Acquire & communicate information • Work with cultural diversity • Participate as a member of a team	0.1.2, 0.1.4, 1.4.1	Beg. Low: 12, 13, 21, 38, 39	4.01, 8.01, 11.06, 15.03, 15.04, 15.06, 15.07, 16.01, 16.02, 16.04, 16.05, 16.06, 16.07, 16.08, 16.09, 16.11	4.01, 8.01, 11.06, 15.02, 15.06, 15.07, 16.01, 16.02, 16.04, 16.05, 16.06, 16.07, 16.08, 16.09, 16.11
• WH-Questions: *Where* • Present continuous tense • Verb: To be • Prepositions of location: *next to, across from, between, on* • There is	• Places & services in the community • Addresses of key community services used (bank, clinic, library, drug store, post office, supermarket) • Different kinds of places where people shop around the world • Interpreting a simple street map	• Identify community resources • Seek & receive information • Gather information • Interact in a way that is courteous • Respect others & value diversity • Cooperate with others • Work together	• Basic skills • Acquire & communicate information • Understand a social system (community) • Work with cultural diversity • See things in the mind's eye • Participate as a member of a team	0.1.2, 0.1.4	*Beg. Literacy:* 5, 11 Beg. Low: 22, 23, 24	5.01, 15.03, 15.04, 15.06, 15.07, 16.01, 16.02, 16.05, 16.06, 16.08, 16.09, 16.11	5.01, 15.02, 15.06, 15.07, 16.01, 16.02, 16.05, 16.06, 16.08, 16.09, 16.11
• Verb: To be • WH-Questions: *What, Where* • Subject pronouns • Adjectives	• Different ways that people in different cultures show their feelings	• Gather information • Identify family relationships • Interact in a way that is friendly • Respect others & value diversity • Cooperate with others • Work together	• Basic skills • Acquire & communicate information • Sociability • Work with cultural diversity • Participate as a member of a team	0.1.2, 0.2.1, 0.2.2, 1.1.4	*Beg. Literacy:* 7 Beg. Low: 6	5.02, 5.03, 14.01, 15.01, 15.02, 15.03, 15.04, 15.05, 15.06, 15.07, 16.01, 16.02, 16.05, 16.06, 16.07, 16.08, 16.10, 16.11	5.02, 5.03, 14.01, 15.01, 15.02, 15.05, 15.06, 15.07, 16.01, 16.02, 16.05, 16.06, 16.07, 16.08, 16.10, 16.11
• Singular/Plural • Articles: *A, an* • There is/There are • Verb: To be • Imperatives	• Listing food stores & restaurants used in the community & foods obtained there • Different kinds of foods people around the world eat	• Manage resources: Identify those resources you have • Meet family needs & responsibilities • Seek & receive assistance • Gather information • Identify community resources • Interact in a way that is courteous • Interact in a way that is helpful • Respect others & value diversity • Cooperate with others • Work together	• Basic skills • Identify resources • Acquire & communicate information • Serve clients/customers • Work with cultural diversity • Participate as a member of a team	0.1.2, 0.1.4, 1.1.7, 1.3.7, 1.3.8, 2.6.4, 4.8.3	*Beg. Literacy:* 5, 14 Beg. Low: 14, 32, 35, 37	5.01, 5.03, 7.06, 7.08, 11.02, 15.03, 15.04, 15.06, 15.07, 16.01, 16.02, 16.05, 16.06, 16.08, 16.09, 16.11	5.01, 5.03, 7.09, 7.11, 11.02, 15.02, 15.06, 15.07, 16.01, 16.02, 16.05, 16.06, 16.08, 16.09, 16.11

Scope and Sequence

LANGUAGE SKILLS & STANDARDS-BASED OBJECTIVES

UNIT	KEY TOPICS	LISTENING & SPEAKING	READING & WRITING	NUMERACY/ MATH
9 **Clothing, Colors, & Shopping** *Page 118*	• Clothing items • Asking for clothing in a store • Colors • Clothing sizes • Problems with clothing • Prices	• Identifying clothing items • Locating clothing items in a store • Listening & identifying clothing items • Identifying colors • Describing what a person is wearing • Expressing clothing size needed to a store salesperson • Expressing problems with clothing • Asking the price of items in a store • Offering assistance to customers as a salesperson • Expressing needs to a salesperson in a store	• Writing plural forms of nouns • Writing missing letters in words • Writing on a chart items of clothing, stores where purchased, & their locations • Reading store display signs with prices • Writing about a favorite clothing item • Reading a clothing store directory to determine location of items	• Numbers in clothing sizes • Prices • Using ordinal numbers to indicate floor of a building
10 **The Bank & the Post Office** *Page 132*	• Bank items • Checks • Making change • Postal items • Obtaining post office services	• Identify bank items & forms • Listening & identifying bank items & forms • Identifying post office items & services • Requesting post office items & services • Paying for goods & services • Giving & receiving correct change during transactions	• Writing information on a chart about banking services used • Reading & writing bank checks • Reading signs in a post office • Identifying return address & mailing address on an envelope • Completing a chart indicating a schedule of opening & closing times • Writing about strategies for controlling expenses & saving money • Interpreting a fast-food menu	• Indicating amount of money on a check • Writing opening & closing times on a schedule • Making change • Subtraction • Identifying prices on a fast-food restaurant menu
11 **Health** *Page 144*	• Parts of the body • Ailments • Medicine • Making a doctor's appointment • Staying healthy • Dosage information on medicine labels	• Identifying parts of the body • Asking about another person's health • Describing ailments, symptoms, & injuries • Listening & identifying ailments, symptoms, & injuries • Indicating what hurts to medical personnel • Asking for & giving advice about over-the-counter medicine • Locating items in a drug store • Using the telephone to make a medical appointment • Expressing sympathy • Calling for an ambulance • Understanding a doctor's medical advice • Repeating information to check understanding • Asking & answering questions about health habits • Understanding a pharmacist's dosage instructions for prescription medicines	• Reading signs in drug store aisles to locate products • Writing information on a chart about pharmacist recommendations for common ailments & symptoms • Reading & writing missing words in a cloze paragraph about staying healthy • Writing survey information about students' health habits on a chart • Understanding dosage instructions on medicine labels • Writing about remedies used for common ailments & symptoms • Reading a drug store directory to determine location of items	• Indicating time when making an appointment • Interpreting numbers in medical advice (e.g., sleep 8 hours, eat 3 meals) • Interpreting numbers in dosage instructions for medicine • Aisle numbers in stores
12 **School** *Page 158*	• School personnel & locations • School subjects • Extracurricular activities • Class schedules	• Identifying school personnel • Identifying school locations • Identifying school subjects • Telling about favorite school subject • Identifying extracurricular activities • Listening & identifying school subjects & extracurricular activities • Describing after-school plans • Talking about a class schedule	• Writing information on a chart about students' favorite school subjects • Writing information on a chart about names of schools in the community, their locations, & their students • Interpreting a class schedule • Writing a description of places & people in your school	• Cardinal & ordinal numbers review • Interpreting numbers in a class schedule (periods, classroom numbers, class times)

CURRICULUM STANDARDS & FRAMEWORKS

BASIC GRAMMAR	COMMUNITY/ CIVICS & CULTURE	EFF	SCANS	CASAS	LAUSD	FLORIDA	
						FOUNDATIONS	**LOW BEGINNING**
• Singular / Plural • Adjectives • Too + adjective	• Listing clothing stores in the community, their locations, & types of clothing purchased there • Different kinds of special clothing people in different cultures wear on special days	• Seek & receive assistance • Identify problems • Identify community resources • Gather information • Understand & work with numbers • Respect others & value diversity • Cooperate with others • Work together	• Basic skills • Identify resources • Acquire & communicate information • Serve clients/customers • Work with cultural diversity • Participate as a member of a team	0.1.2, 0.1.4, 1.1.9, 1.2.1, 1.3.7, 1.3.9, 4.8.3	*Beg. Literacy:* 5, 8, 13, 14 Beg. Low: 14, 31, 32, 33, 34	5.01, 5.03, 8.05, 11.01, 11.03, 11.04, 15.01, 15.03, 15.04, 15.06, 15.07, 16.01, 16.02, 16.05, 16.06, 16.07, 16.08, 16.09, 16.10, 16.11	5.01, 5.03, 8.04, 11.01, 11.04, 15.01, 15.02, 15.06, 15.07, 16.01, 16.02, 16.05, 16.06, 16.07, 16.08, 16.09, 16.11
• WH-Questions: *Where, What, How much* • Want to	• Listing banks & banking services students use • Obtaining services at the post office • Interpreting a posted schedule of opening & closing times at a community location • Different kinds of coins & bills in different countries, & their values	• Meet family needs & responsibilities • Identify community resources • Gather information • Seek & receive assistance • Understand, interpret, & work with numbers • Use math to solve problems & communicate • Manage resources • Respect others & value diversity • Cooperate with others • Work together	• Basic skills • Acquire & communicate information • Allocate money • Self-management • Work with cultural diversity • Participate as a member of a team	0.1.2, 1.3.1, 1.3.3, 1.8.2, 2.4.1, 2.4.2, 2.4.4, 2.5.4, 6.1.2	Beg. Low: 8	5.01, 8.01, 8.05, 8.06, 8.07, 11.01, 11.05, 12.03, 15.03, 15.04, 15.06, 15.07, 16.01, 16.02, 16.05, 16.06, 16.08, 16.09, 16.10, 16.11	5.01, 8.04, 8.05, 8.06, 8.07, 12.03, 15.02, 15.06, 15.07, 16.01, 16.02, 16.05, 16.06, 16.08, 16.09, 16.11
• WH-Questions: *What, Where, How many* • Have / Has • Should • Can • Want to • Past Tense	• Locating products in a drug store • Visiting a local drug store & obtaining pharmacist recommendations for over-the-counter medicine • Calling for an ambulance • Different remedies for common medical problems in different cultures	• Seek & receive assistance • Guide & support others • Gather & use information • Interact in a way that is friendly & courteous • Give direction • Provide for family members' safety & physical needs • Understand, interpret, & work with numbers & symbolic information • Respect others & value diversity • Cooperate with others • Work together	• Basic skills • Acquire & communicate information • Identify resources • Serve clients/customers • Sociability: Demonstrate empathy • Self-management • Work with cultural diversity • Participate as a member of a team	0.1.2, 0.1.4, 1.3.7, 2.1.2, 3.1.1, 3.1.2, 3.1.3, 3.3.1, 3.3.2, 3.3.3, 3.5.9	*Beg. Literacy:* 9 Beg. Low: 12, 21, 32, 43, 44, 45, 46	5.01, 5.02, 5.03, 6.01, 6.04, 7.01, 7.02, 7.03, 7.04, 7.07, 15.03, 15.04, 15.06, 15.07, 16.01, 16.02, 16.05, 16.06, 16.10, 16.11	5.01, 5.02, 6.01, 6.04, 7.01, 7.02, 7.03, 7.04, 7.05, 7.06, 7.10, 10.02, 15.02, 15.06, 15.07, 16.01, 16.02, 16.05, 16.06, 16.10, 16.11
• WH-Questions: *Who, Where, What, Which* • Have	• Listing different types of schools in the community, their locations, & the students who attend • Different types of school buildings & classrooms around the world	• Gather information • Identify community resources • Manage resources: Allocate time • Respect others & value diversity • Cooperate with others • Work together	• Basic skills • Identify resources • Sociability • See things in the mind's eye (Interpret a chart) • Allocate time • Understand a social system (school) • Work with cultural diversity • Participate as a member of a team	0.1.2, 2.5.5	*Beg. Literacy:* 15 Beg. Low: 12, 16, 17	5.01, 5.03, 8.01, 15.03, 15.04, 15.06, 15.07, 16.01, 16.02, 16.04, 16.05, 16.06, 16.08, 16.09, 16.11	5.01, 5.03, 15.02, 15.06, 15.07, 16.02, 16.04, 16.05, 16.06, 16.08, 16.09, 16.11

Scope and Sequence

LANGUAGE SKILLS & STANDARDS-BASED OBJECTIVES

UNIT	KEY TOPICS	LISTENING & SPEAKING	READING & WRITING	NUMERACY/ MATH
13 **Work** *Page 170*	• Occupations • Job skills • Help Wanted signs & want ads • Places at work • Safety warnings & signs • Work schedules & paychecks	• Identifying occupations • Describing occupation & place of work • Expressing job goal during an interview • Listening to job goals & selecting related Help Wanted signs & want ads • Identifying job skills & work activities • Indicating job skills during an interview • Expressing self-confidence during an interview • Calling in sick • Asking the location of workplace departments & facilities • Warning a co-worker of a safety hazard • Interpreting warning & safety signs at work	• Reading Help Wanted signs • Writing missing letters in words • Reading want ads • Filling out a job application form • Writing information on a chart about students' job skills • Interpreting a workplace floor plan diagram • Reading & copying Help Wanted signs in the community • Interpreting workplace warning & safety signs • Reading a work schedule • Reading a paycheck & pay stub • Reading & writing missing numbers in a cloze paragraph • Writing a description of a workplace • Indicating job skills on a checklist	• Identifying telephone numbers in classified ads • Interpreting times in a work schedule • Interpreting numbers, dates, & dollar amounts on a paycheck & pay stub
14 **Transportation** *Page 188*	• Locating places • Asking for & giving directions • Types of public transportation • Traffic signs • Driving safety warnings	• Identifying modes of travel • Getting someone's attention politely • Asking for & giving directions to a place • Listening & identifying correct locations on a map • Asking for & giving information about local transportation & routes • Listening & identifying correct destination signs on buses & trains & correct street signs • Asking passengers on local transportation where to get off for a destination • Asking & telling about about modes of transportation used • Warning a driver about an upcoming traffic sign • Asking & telling about a bus schedule • Repeating to confirm information	• Interpreting a simple street map • Reading destination signs on buses & trains • Reading street signs & station signs to locate destination • Writing classroom survey results on a chart • Writing information on a chart about public transportation used • Interpreting traffic signs • Drawing traffic signs & writing their meanings • Interpreting a bus route schedule • Writing about how you get to places in the community	• Identifying bus numbers • Interpreting numbers on street signs & traffic signs • Counting student responses to a survey & entering the information on a chart • Interpreting times on a bus schedule
15 **Recreation & Entertainment** *Page 202*	• Recreation & entertainment activities • Expressing likes • Expressing future plans • Telling about past activities • Calendars & schedules	• Asking & telling about recreation & entertainment activities • Expressing likes • Listening & identifying recreation & entertainment activities • Asking & telling about plans to do a future activity • Asking & telling about a past activity • Listening & distinguishing present & past tense statements	• Writing missing letters in words • Writing survey information about students' free time activities on a chart • Writing information on a chart about places for recreation & entertainment • Interpreting a monthly calendar with activities listed • Reading a paragrapn with accompanying graphic • Writing about plans for next weekend • Reading personal schedule information on a daily calendar	• Counting student responses to a survey & entering information on a chart • Using a calendar • Interpreting time information on a daily calendar schedule

CURRICULUM STANDARDS & FRAMEWORKS

BASIC GRAMMAR	COMMUNITY/ CIVICS & CULTURE	EFF	SCANS	CASAS	LAUSD	FLORIDA	
						FOUNDATIONS	LOW BEGINNING
• Verb: To be • Can • WH-Questions: *What, Where* • Prepositions of location: *across from, next to, between*	• Finding & interpreting Help Wanted signs in the community • Discussing different types of jobs & workplaces in the community • Men's & women's jobs in different cultures, & changes that are occurring	• Identify goals • Develop & express sense of self • Gather information • Seek & receive assistance • Give direction • Take responsibility for assuring work safety • Understand, interpret, & work with numbers • Respect others & value diversity • Cooperate with others • Work together	• Basic skills • Identify human resources (occupations, work skills) • Identify goal-relevant activities • Self-management: Assess self accurately • Self-esteem • Understand a social system (workplace) • See things in the mind's eye (Interpret a diagram; Interpret a sign with symbols; Draw a sign with symbols) • Work with cultural diversity • Participate as a member of a team	0.1.2, 4.1.2, 4.1.3, 4.1.6, 4.1.8, 4.3.1, 4.3.3	*Beg. Literacy:* 5, 10 Beg. Low: 11, 12, 14, 48, 49, 50, 51, 52, 53, 54, 56	1.01, 1.02, 1.03, 1.04, 1.07, 2.01, 2.02, 2.03, 2.04, 2.05, 3.03, 5.01, 5.02, 10.01, 15.03, 15.04, 15.05, 15.06, 15.07, 16.01, 16.02, 16.03, 16.05, 16.06, 16.08, 16.09, 16.11	1.01, 1.02, 1.03, 1.04, 1.07, 2.01, 2.02, 2.03, 2.04, 2.05, 3.03, 5.01, 5.02, 10.01, 15.02, 15.05, 15.06, 15.07, 16.02, 16.03, 16.05, 16.06, 16.08, 16.09, 16.11
• WH-Questions: *How, Where* • Imperatives • Prepositions of location: *across from, between, next to, on the left, on the right* • Exclamations	• Asking the location of places in the community • Interpreting a simple street map • Asking for information about public transportation routes • Listing places in the community accessed by public transportation, modes of transportation used, route numbers, & locations • Interpreting traffic signs • Interpreting a bus route schedule • Transportation in different places around the world	• Give direction • Seek & receive assistance • Interact in a way that is friendly, courteous, & helpful • Gather information • Identify community resources • Guide others • Understand, interpret, & work with numbers • Respect others & value diversity • Cooperate with others • Work together	• Basic skills • Acquire & communicate information • See things in the mind's eye (Interpret a map) • Identify resources • Sociability: Demonstrate understanding, friendliness • Work with cultural diversity • Participate as a member of a team	0.1.2, 0.1.3, 0.1.6, 1.9.1, 1.9.4, 2.2.1, 2.2.2, 2.2.3, 2.2.4, 2.5.4	*Beg. Literacy:* 5, 10 Beg. Low: 11, 13, 23, 24, 42, 48, 49	5.01, 9.01, 9.02, 9.03, 9.04, 15.03, 15.04, 15.06, 15.07, 16.01, 16.02, 16.05, 16.06, 16.08, 16.09	5.01, 9.02, 9.03, 9.04, 9.05, 15.02, 15.06, 15.07, 16.02, 16.05, 16.06, 16.08, 16.09
• Like to • Future: Going to • Past tense	• Listing places for recreation & entertainment in the community • Different ways people in different cultures spend their free time	• Interact in a way that is friendly • Gather information • Identify community resources • Manage resources: Allocate time • Plan: Develop an organized approach of activities & objectives • Plan: Set a goal • Respect others & value diversity • Cooperate with others • Work together	• Basic skills • Sociability: Demonstrate friendliness • Acquire & communicate information • Identify goal-relevant activities • Identify resources • Self-management • Work with cultural diversity • Participate as a member of a team	0.1.2, 0.1.4, 0.2.4, 2.6.1, 3.5.8, 3.5.9	Beg. Low: 12, 13, 14	3.03, 5.01, 5.03, 8.01, 14.07, 15.03, 15.04, 15.06, 15.07, 16.01, 16.02, 16.05, 16.06, 16.08, 16.09, 16.11	3.03, 5.01, 5.03, 14.07, 15.02, 15.06, 15.07, 16.01, 16.02, 16.05, 16.06, 16.08, 16.09, 16.11

Foundations is an all-skills, standards-based program for beginning-literacy and low-beginning learners of English. Its simple format, easy-to-use photo dictionary lessons, and dynamic communication activities offer students a lively and motivating introduction to basic English for essential life skills. The program builds a language *foundation* to prepare students for future success at the Book 1 level of instruction. For additional vocabulary enrichment, *Foundations* correlates unit-by-unit with the *Word by Word Basic* Picture Dictionary.

An Overview

Photo Dictionary Lessons

Each unit of *Foundations* begins with a two-page Vocabulary Preview in an easy-to-use photo dictionary format. These lessons offer students a clear visual reference and study tool for previewing and mastering more than 350 key words that occur in the units—especially helpful preparation for the low-beginning learner.

Two-Page Lesson Format

The core lessons in each unit follow a convenient two-page lesson format that is consistent and predictable and that provides sufficient practice for students to achieve the lesson objectives. This format is specifically designed to provide a successful learning experience for students with limited prior experience using a textbook.

Guided Conversations

Guided conversations are the dialogs and exercises that are the essential learning devices in *Foundations*. Model conversations depict situations in which people use the key vocabulary of each lesson. In the exercises that follow, pairs of students create their own conversations by placing new vocabulary items into the framework of the model. Highlighted words in color and "skeletal dialogs" with blanks help students focus on key vocabulary and practice new conversations.

Follow-Up Exercises and Activities

After each lesson's guided conversation practice, follow-up exercises and activities provide all-skills practice and lively learning through action.

- **Language in Motion** activities get students moving around the classroom as they pantomime actions, ask each other questions, gather information, and do other movement activities.

- **Games** motivate active learning through small-group and full-class practice designed to stimulate classroom interaction.

- **Writing activities** offer basic practice with authentic life-skill writing tasks.

- **Listening exercises** develop students' aural comprehension skills. (An audio program is available, and listening scripts are provided in the appendix.)

- **Mini grammar lessons** offer practice with key grammatical structures. (Grammar is not emphasized in *Foundations*; it is highlighted when basic structures are needed for communication practice.)

- **Community Connections** activities introduce civics topics related to community life and help students connect to community services.

- **Numbers lessons** in every unit provide a careful introduction to basic numeracy and math skills.

- **Different Cultures, Different Ways** sections highlight cross-cultural differences.

- **Language Experience Journal** writing activities prompt students to write basic sentences to apply each unit's vocabulary and topics to their own lives.

Unit Activities

Each unit ends with a series of activities designed to reinforce and build upon the language skills in the preceding lessons.

- **Different Cultures, Different Ways** sections provide photos from around the world to stimulate cross-cultural discussions about how people's lives are different in other countries and cultures.

- **Information Gap** activities promote teamwork as students work in pairs to complete tasks by sharing information and cooperating.

- **Vocabulary lists** and **Language Skill checklists** help students review words they have learned and keep track of the skills they are developing.

- **Full-page illustrations** stimulate a range of vocabulary review activities and games for individual students, pairs, small groups, and the entire class.

Suggested Teaching Strategies

We encourage you, in using *Foundations*, to develop approaches and strategies that are compatible with your own teaching style and the needs and abilities of your students. You may find it helpful to incorporate some of the following suggestions. More specific step-by-step instructions for all lessons are provided in the *Foundations* Teacher's Guide.

Vocabulary Preview (Photo Dictionary lessons)

1. **PREVIEW:** Activate students' prior knowledge of the vocabulary by having them look at the illustrations and identify the words they already know.

2. **PRESENT:** Point to each illustration or say its number, say the word, and have the class repeat it chorally and individually. (You can also play the word list on the Audio Program.) Check students' understanding and pronunciation of the vocabulary.

3. **PRACTICE:** Have students practice as a class, in pairs, or in small groups. Say or write a word, and have students point to the item in their books or tell the number. Or, point to an illustration in the book or give the number, and have students say the word.

(The Teacher's Guide suggests additional activities and games customized for each Vocabulary Preview Lesson.)

Guided Conversations

1. **SETTING THE SCENE:** Have students look at the model photograph in the book. Set the scene: Who are the people? What is the situation?

2. **LISTENING:** With books closed, have students listen to the model conversation—presented by you, by a pair of students, or on the audio program. Check students' understanding of the situation and the vocabulary.

3. **CLASS PRACTICE:** With books still closed, model each line and have the whole class practice in unison.

4. **READING:** With books open, have students follow along as two students present the model.

5. **PAIR PRACTICE:** In pairs, have students practice the model conversation.

6. **THE SKELETAL DIALOG:** Write the "skeletal dialog" on the board. Fill in the replacement from Exercise 1 to show students how the guided conversation method works. Call on a few pairs of students to practice the new Exercise 1 dialog using the skeletal framework on the board.

7. **VOCABULARY PRESENTATION:** Present the new vocabulary words in the exercises. Point to the photograph of each item, say the word, and have the class repeat it chorally and individually. Check students' understanding and pronunciation of the vocabulary. (You can also use the Vocabulary Preview lesson at the beginning of the unit if it contains these new words.)

8. **EXERCISE PRACTICE:** (optional) Have pairs of students simultaneously practice all the exercises.

9. **EXERCISE PRESENTATIONS:** Call on pairs of students to present their conversations to the class.

Community Connections

Have students do the activity individually, in pairs, or in small groups and then report back to the class.

Different Cultures, Different Ways

Have students first work in pairs or small groups, reacting to the photographs and responding to the questions. Then have students share with the class what they have talked about.

Put It Together!

In these paired information gap activities, Student A has information that Student B doesn't have, and vice versa. Students ask each other questions in order to fill in the missing information.

Language Experience Journal

Have students begin a Language Experience Journal in a composition notebook. Depending on your students' writing abilities, either have them write in their journals or dictate sentences for you to write. Then students should read what they have written to a classmate. (If time permits, you may also want to write a response in each student's journal, reacting to what the student has written.) If you are keeping portfolios of students' work, these journal entries serve as excellent examples of students' progress in learning to write in English.

Talk About It! (Full-Page Illustrations)

Use the richly-detailed illustration to review the vocabulary and conversations in the unit. (Color overhead transparencies of these illustrations are also available.) Have students first work in pairs or small groups to talk about the illustration and answer the questions posed at the bottom of the page. Then discuss as a class. Students may enjoy practicing conversations based on the characters and situations and then presenting their conversations to the class. The Teacher's Guide suggests a variety of activities and games customized for each full-page illustration lesson.

While conveying to you the substance of *Foundations*, we hope that we have also conveyed the spirit: that instruction in basic language, vocabulary, and life skills can be dynamic and interactive . . . responsive to beginning-literacy and low-beginning students' differing learning styles . . . relevant to our students' lives . . . and fun!

Steven J. Molinsky
Bill Bliss

Personal Information & Family

Vocabulary Preview

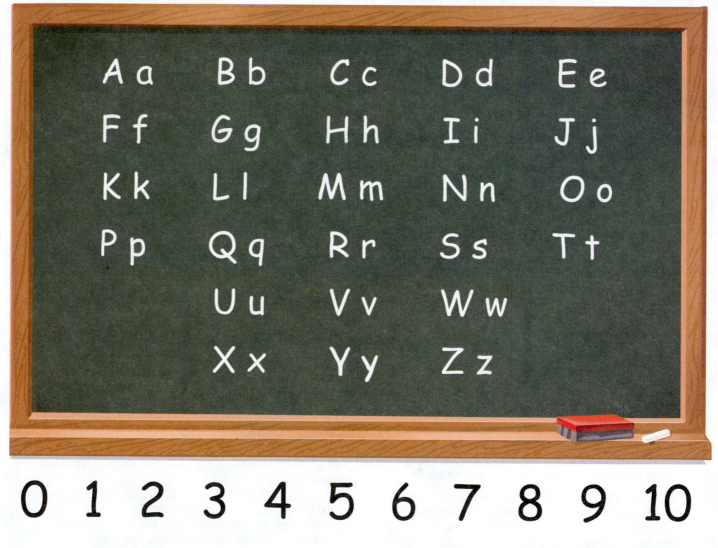

Aa Bb Cc Dd Ee
Ff Gg Hh Ii Jj
Kk Ll Mm Nn Oo
Pp Qq Rr Ss Tt
Uu Vv Ww
Xx Yy Zz

0 1 2 3 4 5 6 7 8 9 10

| 0 zero | 1 one | 3 three | 5 five | 7 seven | 9 nine |
| | 2 two | 4 four | 6 six | 8 eight | 10 ten |

Goals

1 name	**5** apartment number	**9** telephone number
2 first name	**6** city	**10** cell phone number
3 last name	**7** state	**11** e-mail address
4 address	**8** zip code	**12** social security number

A. Hello. My name is **Hung Tran**.

B. Hi. I'm **Gloria Hernandez**. Nice to meet you.

A. Nice to meet you, too.

Practice the conversation with a partner. Use your first and last names.

A. Hello. My name is _____ _____.

B. Hi. I'm _____ _____. Nice to meet you.

A. Nice to meet you, too.

Language in *Motion*

Move around the classroom. Introduce yourself to all the students.

Memory Game

Victor Silva.

Victor Silva, Rosa Fernandez.

Victor Silva, Rosa Fernandez, Daniel Teferra.

Stand in a circle. Say the names of all the students.

Names and the Alphabet

Circle the letters in your first name.

Ⓐ B Ⓒ D E F G H I J K Ⓛ M N Ⓞ P Q Ⓡ Ⓢ T U V W X Y Z

Write your first name.

CARLOS
_____
FIRST NAME

| C | A | R | L | O | S | | | | | | | | | | |

First Name

| C | A | R | L | O | S | | | | | | | | | |

First Name

Circle the letters in your first name.

A B C D E F G H I J K L M N O P Q R S T U V W X Y Z

Write your first name.

_____
FIRST NAME

| | | | | | | | | | | | | | | | |

First Name

| | | | | | | | | | | | | | |

First Name

Circle the letters in your last name.

A B C D E F G H I J K L M N O P Q R S T U V W X Y Z

Write your last name.

_____
LAST NAME

| | | | | | | | | | | | | | | | |

Last Name

| | | | | | | | | | | | | | |

Last Name

A. **What's your last name?**

B. Sanchez.

A. **How do you spell it?**

B. S–A–N–C–H–E–Z.

Practice conversations with a partner.

A. What's your last name?

B. _____.

A. How do you spell it?

B. _____.

Listening 🎧 Listen and circle.

1. K–W–A–N   (P–H–A–N)
2. B–L–A–C–K   D–R–A–K–E
3. K–E–L–T–O–N   C–L–A–Y–T–O–N
4. G–R–E–E–N   L–E–E–S
5. B–R–E–N–N–E–R   K–R–A–M–E–R
6. S–A–N–C–H–E–Z   S–A–N–D–E–R–S

Missing Letters

Write the missing letters.

A B C D E F G H I J K L M N O P Q R S T U V W X Y Z

What word do the letters spell?   N A M E

Write the missing letters.

__ B C D E F G H I J K __ M N O P Q R __ __ U V W X Y Z

What word do the letters spell?   __ __ __ __

Write the missing letters.

A B C D E __ G H __ J K L M N O P Q __ __ __ U V W X Y Z

What word do the letters spell?   __ __ __ __ __

Language in *Motion*

Move around the classroom. Ask six students.
Write their first and last names.

What's your first name?
How do you spell it?

What's your last name?
How do you spell it?

	First Names	Last Names
1.		
2.		
3.		
4.		
5.		
6.		

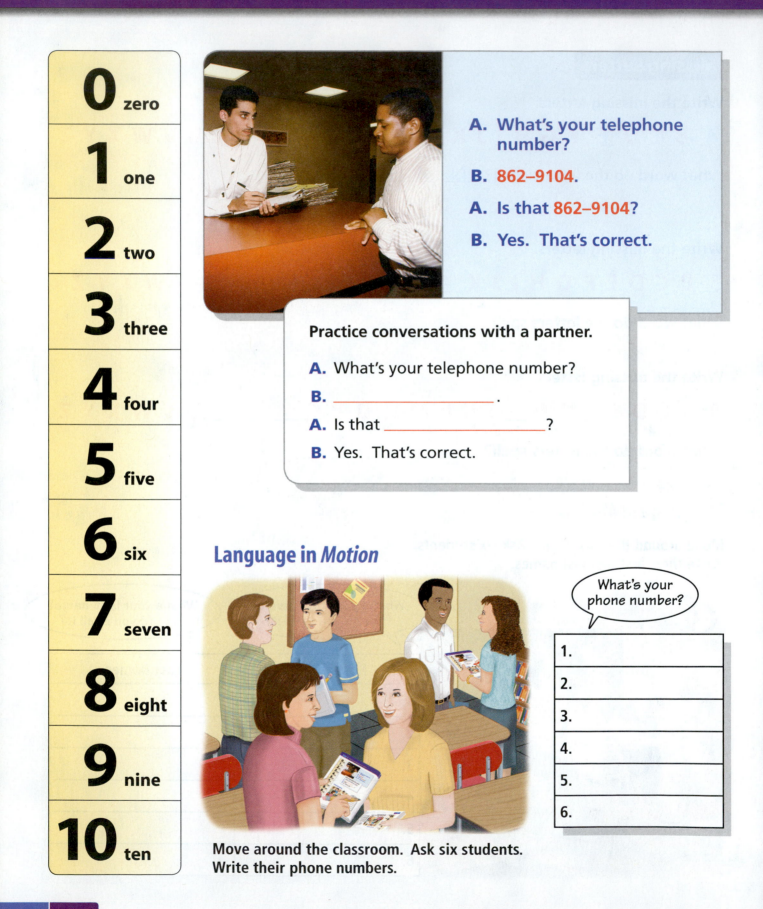

0 zero	
1 one	
2 two	
3 three	
4 four	
5 five	
6 six	
7 seven	
8 eight	
9 nine	
10 ten	

A. What's your telephone number?

B. 862–9104.

A. Is that 862–9104?

B. Yes. That's correct.

Practice conversations with a partner.

A. What's your telephone number?

B. _____ .

A. Is that _____?

B. Yes. That's correct.

Language in *Motion*

What's your phone number?

1.	
2.	
3.	
4.	
5.	
6.	

Move around the classroom. Ask six students.
Write their phone numbers.

Missing Numbers   Write the missing numbers.

0   1   2   3   <u>4</u>   5   6   ___   8   ___   10

0   1   ___   3   4   ___   6   7   ___   9   ___

___   ___   ___   ___   ___   5   ___   ___   ___   ___   10

Listening

Listen and circle.

1. (249–1115)   245–1119
2. 463–9112   463–9221
3. 948–6137   984–1673
4. 671–2058   671–2098
5. 728–0303   728–3030
6. 837–1284   837–1234

Matching

Match the words and numbers.

1. four   1
2. nine   8
3. one   4
4. eight   3
5. seven   9
6. three   7

Community Connections

Write these important telephone numbers.

Police:

_____

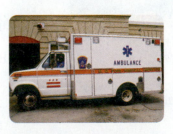

Ambulance:

_____

Fire:

_____

Poison Control Center:

_____

9

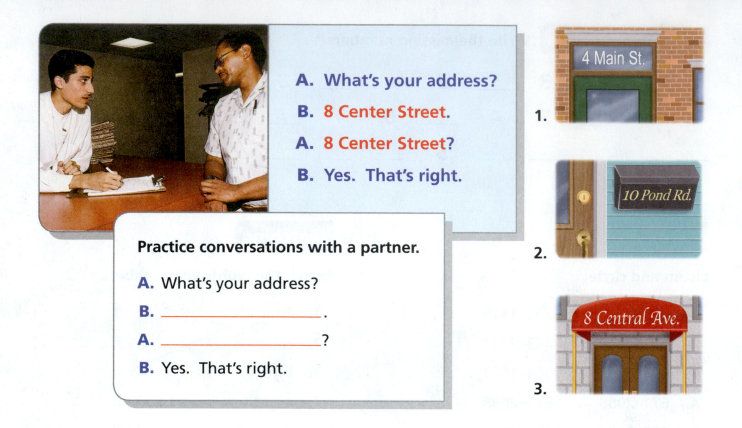

A. What's your address?

B. 8 Center Street.

A. 8 Center Street?

B. Yes. That's right.

Practice conversations with a partner.

A. What's your address?

B. _____ .

A. _____ ?

B. Yes. That's right.

1. 4 Main St.

2. 10 Pond Rd.

3. 8 Central Ave.

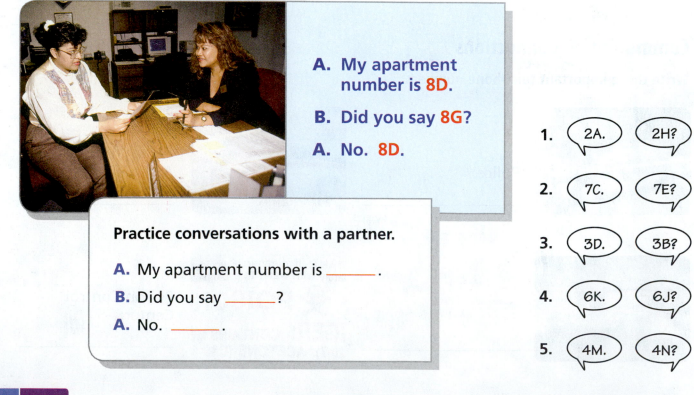

A. My apartment number is 8D.

B. Did you say 8G?

A. No. 8D.

Practice conversations with a partner.

A. My apartment number is _____ .

B. Did you say _____ ?

A. No. _____ .

1. 2A.   2H?

2. 7C.   7E?

3. 3D.   3B?

4. 6K.   6J?

5. 4M.   4N?

Pronunciation

Practice the apartment numbers.

1A – 1H

3B – 3D

8M – 8N

5P – 5B

2D – 2T

9C – 9G

4J – 4A

Listening

Circle the apartment number you hear.

1.   6C   6D
2.   9A   9J
3.   1E   1G
4.   10K   10J
5.   2B   2D
6.   8C   8G
7.   3B   3E

Form Information

What's the name of your city?   _____

What's the name of your state?   _____

What's the abbreviation of your state? ___ ___

What's your zip code?   _____

Some Abbreviations	
California	CA
Florida	FL
Illinois	IL
New York	NY
Texas	TX

Fill Out the Form

NAME
First   Last

ADDRESS
Number   Street

City   State   Zip Code

TELEPHONE
Area Code   Number

CELL PHONE
Area Code   Number

E-MAIL

A. This is my **wife**.

B. Nice to meet you.

C. Nice to meet you, too.

A. This is my **husband**.

B. Nice to meet you.

C. Nice to meet you, too.

Practice conversations in groups of three.

A. This is my _____.

B. Nice to meet you.

C. Nice to meet you, too.

1. mother

2. father

3. daughter

4. son

5. sister

6. brother

7. grandmother

8. grandfather

A Family Tree **Finish the sentences.**

Rosa

Ben

Maria

Frank

David

Jenny

1. Rosa is Ben's _____wife_____.
2. Ben is Rosa's _____.
3. Maria is Rosa and Ben's _____.
4. Maria is David and Jenny's _____.
5. Frank is David and Jenny's _____.
6. David is Jenny's _____.
7. Jenny is David's _____.
8. Rosa is David and Jenny's _____.
9. Ben is David and Jenny's _____.

Your Family Members

What family members live in your home?

_____

What other family members live in this country?

_____

What family members live in other countries? Where?

_____

More Family Vocabulary

aunt
uncle
niece
nephew
cousin
granddaughter
grandson

Language in *Motion*

Practice the conversation.

A. Who is this?

B. This is my grandfather.

A. What's his name?

B. His name is Gustavo.

**Bring in family photos.
Move around the classroom.
Ask and answer questions.**

A. Who is this?
B. This is my _____.
A. What's his/her name?
B. His/Her name is _____.

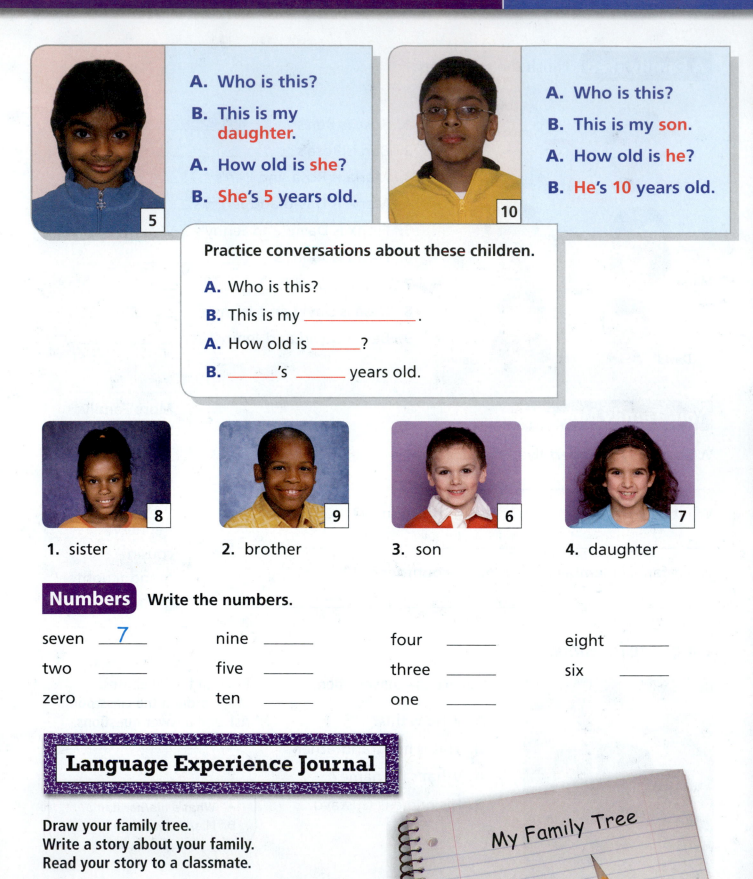

A. Who is this?

B. This is my **daughter**.

A. How old is **she**?

B. **She's 5** years old.

5

A. Who is this?

B. This is my **son**.

A. How old is **he**?

B. **He's 10** years old.

10

Practice conversations about these children.

A. Who is this?

B. This is my _____.

A. How old is _____?

B. _____'s _____ years old.

8

9

6

7

1. sister

2. brother

3. son

4. daughter

Numbers Write the numbers.

seven ___7___   nine _____   four _____   eight _____

two _____   five _____   three _____   six _____

zero _____   ten _____   one _____

Language Experience Journal

Draw your family tree.
Write a story about your family.
Read your story to a classmate.

My Family Tree

Different Cultures Different Ways

People greet each other in different ways in different cultures.

Some people shake hands.

Some people hug.

Some people kiss.

Some people bow.

In your culture, how do people greet friends?
How do people greet each other at work?
How do children greet their parents?

PUT IT TOGETHER : PART A

Work with a partner. One person looks at this page. The other person looks at page 16. Ask each other questions and fill out the form.

INFORMATION GAP ACTIVITY

What's the person's first name?

Cathy. What's her last name?

Kwan.

NAME	Kwan	
	First	Last

ADDRESS	8	
	Number	Street

	Long Beach		90815
	City	State	Zip Code

TELEPHONE _____

SOCIAL SECURITY NUMBER 062-83-4796

INFORMATION GAP ACTIVITY

Work with a partner. One person looks at this page. The other person looks at page 15. Ask each other questions and fill out the form.

NAME _Cathy_____
First   Last

ADDRESS ____Center Street_____
Number   Street

_____CA_____
City   State   Zip Code

TELEPHONE _(310) 472-9813_____

SOCIAL SECURITY NUMBER _____

What's the person's first name?

Cathy. What's her last name?

Kwan.

VOCABULARY FOUNDATIONS

Hello	wife
Hi	husband
	mother
name	father
first name	daughter
last name	son
address	sister
apartment number	brother
city	grandmother
state	grandfather
zip code	aunt
telephone number	uncle
cell phone number	niece
e-mail address	nephew
social security number	cousin
	granddaughter
spell	grandson

LANGUAGE SKILL FOUNDATIONS

I can . . .
- ☐ introduce myself
- ☐ spell my name
- ☐ give my telephone number
- ☐ identify emergency telephone numbers
- ☐ give my address
- ☐ introduce family members
- ☐ check my understanding
- ☐ give correction
- ☐ print alphabet letters
- ☐ use and write numbers 0–10
- ☐ fill out a simple form
- ☐ draw and describe my family tree
- ☐ compare greetings in different cultures

What's your name?
What's your address?
What's your phone number?

Talk About It! ▶▶▶ What's happening? What are these people saying?

17

Unit 2

The Classroom

Vocabulary Preview

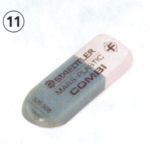

1 board	**5** calculator	**9** computer
2 book	**6** chair	**10** desk
3 bookshelf	**7** chalk	**11** eraser
4 bulletin board	**8** clock	**12** globe

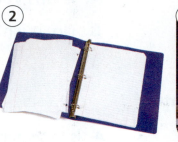

1 map	**5** pencil	**9** table
2 notebook	**6** ruler	**10** teacher
3 overhead projector	**7** screen	**11** TV
4 pen	**8** student	**12** wall

A. Is this your **pen**?

B. Yes, it is. Thank you.

A. Is this your **pen**?

B. No, it isn't.

Practice conversations with a partner.

A. Is this your _____?

B. Yes, it is. Thank you.

A. Is this your _____?

B. No, it isn't.

1. pencil

2. book

3. notebook

4. ruler

5. eraser

6. calculator

Matching

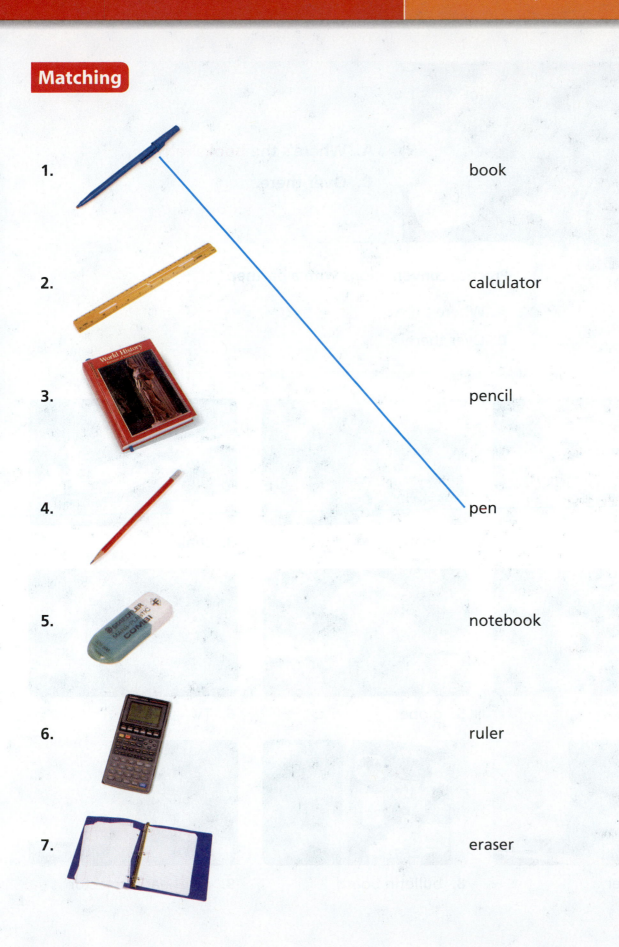

1.

2.

3.

4.

5.

6.

7.

book

calculator

pencil

pen

notebook

ruler

eraser

A. Where's the bookshelf?

B. Over there.

Practice conversations with a partner.

A. Where's the _____?

B. Over there.

1. desk

2. board

3. chalk

4. map

5. globe

6. TV

7. computer

8. bulletin board

9. overhead projector

Listening  Listen and write the number under the correct picture.

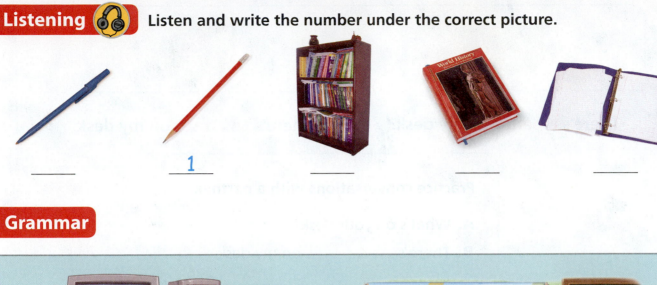

_____ 1 _____ _____ _____

Grammar

The computer is **on** the table.

The map is **next to** the board.

Circle the correct answer.

1. The globe is [on] / next to the bookshelf.

2. The pen is on / next to the pencil.

3. The calculator is on / next to the ruler.

4. The eraser is on / next to the book.

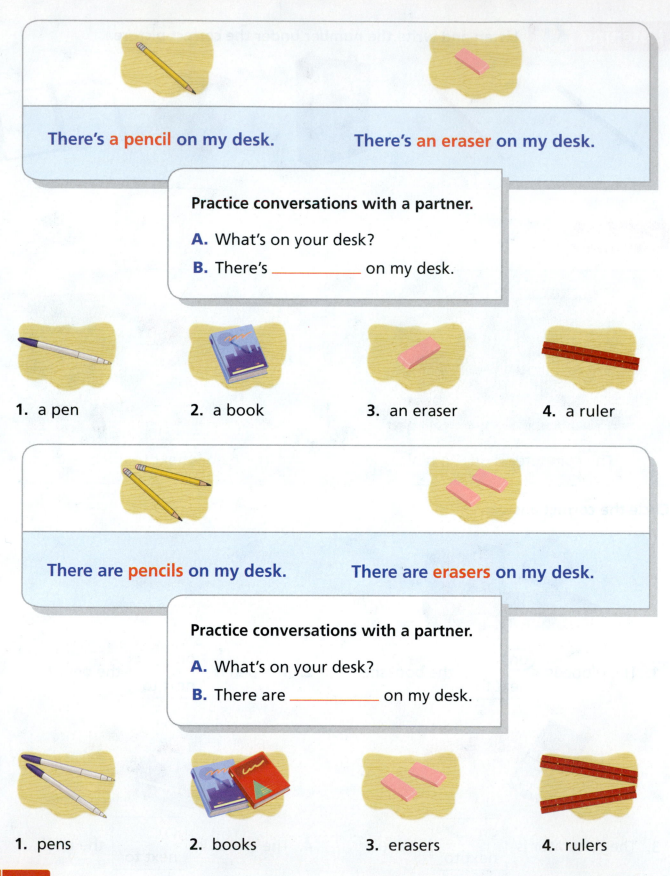

There's **a pencil** on my desk.   There's **an eraser** on my desk.

Practice conversations with a partner.

A. What's on your desk?

B. There's _____ on my desk.

1. a pen   2. a book   3. an eraser   4. a ruler

There are **pencils** on my desk.   There are **erasers** on my desk.

Practice conversations with a partner.

A. What's on your desk?

B. There are _____ on my desk.

1. pens   2. books   3. erasers   4. rulers

Grammar Write the correct word.

a	an	are

1. There's ____a____ computer in my classroom.
2. There ___are___ desks in my classroom.
3. There's _____ globe in my classroom.
4. There's _____ overhead projector in my classroom.
5. There _____ bulletin boards in my classroom.

There's	There are

6. ___There's___ a TV in my classroom.
7. ___There are___ books in my classroom.
8. _____ a teacher in my classroom.
9. _____ students in my classroom.
10. _____ rulers in my classroom.

Memory Game

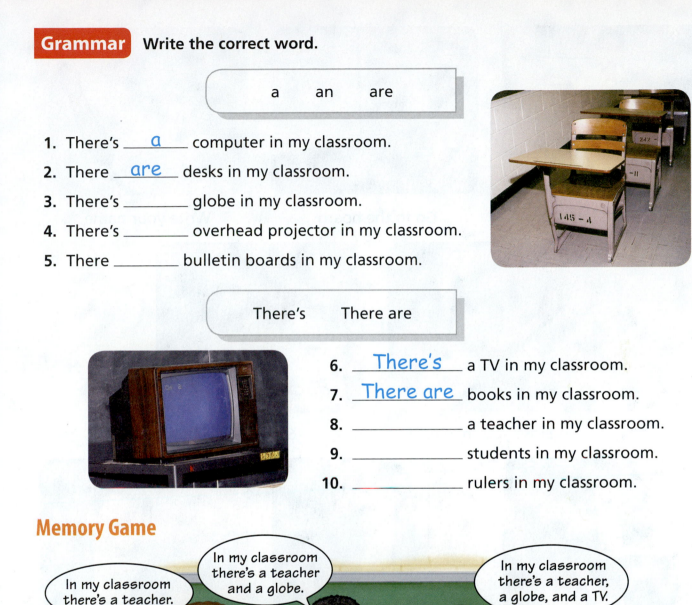

In my classroom there's a teacher.

In my classroom there's a teacher and a globe.

In my classroom there's a teacher, a globe, and a TV.

Stand in a circle. Repeat the things you hear. Add something new.

Community ⊙ Connections

Visit a classroom in another school. Make a list of all the things in the classroom.

Stand up.

Go to the board.

Write your name.

Erase your name.

Sit down.

Take out your book.

Open your book.

Raise your hand.

Close your book.

Put away your book.

Matching

1. Sit    your name.
2. Stand   down.
3. Write   your book.
4. Open   up.

5. Go to   your pen.
6. Erase   your hand.
7. Put away   your name.
8. Raise   the door.

Listening

Listen and write the number under the correct picture.

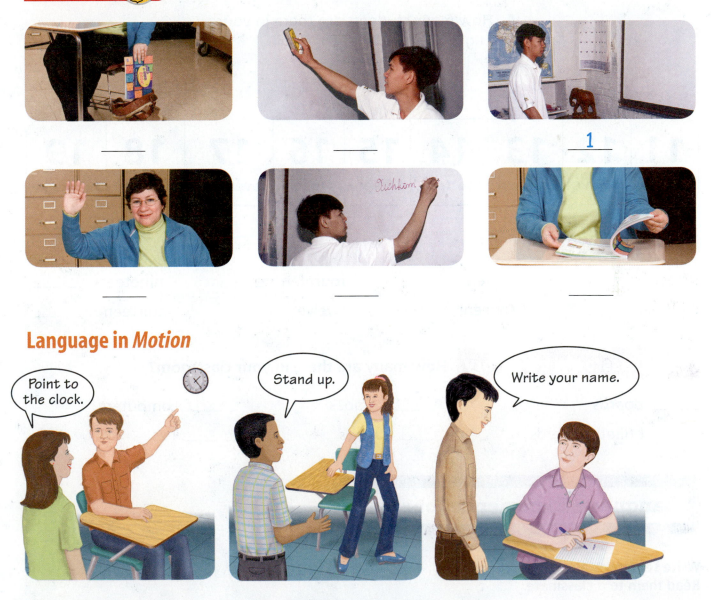

_____   _____   1

_____   _____   _____

Language in *Motion*

Point to the clock.

Stand up.

Write your name.

Practice with a classmate. Give and follow instructions in this lesson.

A. How many students are there in your English class?

B. Eleven.

Practice conversations with these numbers.

A. How many students are there in your English class?

B. _____.

11	12	13	14	15	16	17	18	19
eleven	twelve	thirteen	fourteen	fifteen	sixteen	seventeen	eighteen	nineteen

Numbers Write the numbers.

fifteen _15_   eleven _____   fourteen _____   nineteen _____

eighteen _____   sixteen _____   twelve _____   thirteen _____

Your Classroom Inventory How many are there in your classroom?

_____ boards   _____ globes   _____ computers

_____ bulletin boards   _____ maps   _____ TVs

Language Experience Journal

Write sentences about your classroom.
Read them to a classmate.

My Classroom

Different Cultures / Different Ways

Classrooms are different around the world.

Tell about classrooms in other countries.
How are they different from classrooms here?

PUT IT TOGETHER : PART A

Work with a partner. You're in two different classrooms. Ask each other about objects in your classrooms.

Your Classroom		Your Partner's Classroom
No	bulletin board	Yes
Yes	map	___
No	bookshelf	___
Yes	TV	___
No	globe	___
Yes	screen	___
No	overhead projector	___
Yes	computer	___

INFORMATION GAP ACTIVITY

Is there a bulletin board in your classroom?

Yes, there is. Is there a bulletin board in YOUR classroom?

No, there isn't.

INFORMATION GAP ACTIVITY

Work with a partner. You're in two different classrooms. Ask each other about objects in your classrooms.

Your Classroom		Your Partner's Classroom
Yes	bulletin board	<u>No</u>
No	map	____
Yes	bookshelf	____
No	TV	____
Yes	globe	____
No	screen	____
No	overhead projector	____
Yes	computer	____

VOCABULARY FOUNDATIONS

board	screen
book	student
bookshelf	table
bulletin board	teacher
calculator	TV
chair	wall
chalk	
clock	stand up
computer	sit down
desk	write
eraser	erase
globe	open
map	close
notebook	take out
overhead projector	put away
pen	raise
pencil	go
ruler	point

LANGUAGE SKILL FOUNDATIONS

I can . . .

- ☐ identify classroom items
- ☐ ask about someone's possessions
- ☐ express gratitude
- ☐ ask about location
- ☐ tell the location
- ☐ describe my classroom
- ☐ follow classroom instructions
- ☐ give classroom instructions
- ☐ use and write numbers 11–19
- ☐ compare classrooms in different cultures

Vocabulary Preview

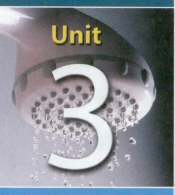
1

2

3

4

5

6

7

8

9

10

11

12

13

14

15

1 get up	**5** get dressed	**9** go to school	**13** watch TV
2 take a shower	**6** eat breakfast	**10** come home	**14** get undressed
3 brush my teeth	**7** go to work	**11** cook dinner	**15** go to bed
4 comb my hair	**8** eat lunch	**12** read	

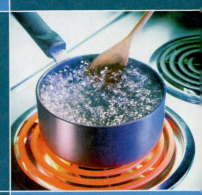

1	make breakfast	**5**	wash the dishes	**9**	walk the dog	**13** play the guitar
2	make lunch	**6**	do the laundry	**10**	study	**14** play basketball
3	make dinner	**7**	iron	**11**	exercise	
4	clean	**8**	feed the baby	**12**	listen to music	

A. What do you do every day?

B. I get up, I brush my teeth, and I comb my hair.

Practice conversations with a partner.
Use everyday activities on page 32.

A. What do you do every day?

B. I _____, I _____, and I _____.

Memory Game

Every day I get up.

Every day I get up and I take a shower.

Every day I get up, I take a shower, and I get dressed.

Stand in a circle. Repeat the activities you hear. Add a new activity.

Matching

1. watch	my teeth		**5.** comb	to work
2. brush	dressed		**6.** eat	my hair
3. get	a shower		**7.** go	breakfast
4. take	TV		**8.** get	undressed

Listening

Listen and write the number under the correct picture.

_____   __1__   _____   _____   _____

What's the Order?

1. __3__ I eat dinner.
     __2__ I eat lunch.
     __1__ I eat breakfast.

2. _____ I go to work.
     _____ I get up.
     _____ I take a shower.

3. _____ I come home.
     _____ I go to work.
     _____ I eat breakfast.

4. _____ I comb my hair.
     _____ I eat lunch.
     _____ I get up.

5. _____ I go to bed.
     _____ I go to school.
     _____ I get dressed.

6. _____ I get up.
     _____ I go to bed.
     _____ I get undressed.

A. Hi! What are you doing?

B. I'm cleaning. How about you?

A. I'm making breakfast.

Practice conversations with a partner. Talk about these activities.

A. Hi! What are you doing?

B. I'm _____. How about you?

A. I'm _____.

studying

exercising

feeding the baby

doing the laundry

washing the dishes

listening to music

ironing

playing the guitar

Matching

1. I'm listening to   lunch.
2. I'm making   baby.
3. I'm cleaning   music.
4. I'm feeding the   the house.

5. I'm making   guitar.
6. I'm washing the   dinner.
7. I'm watching   TV.
8. I'm playing the   dishes.

Listening

Listen and write the number under the correct picture.

_____

_____

_____

_____

  1

_____

_____

_____

Language in *Motion*

Pantomime an activity. Other students guess the activity.

You're exercising.

You're ironing.

A. **What do you do every day?**

B. **I read.**

A. **What are you doing right now?**

B. **I'm reading.**

Practice conversations with a partner.
Talk about these activities.

A. What do you do every day?

B. I _____.

A. What are you doing right now?

B. I'm _____.

1. clean
   cleaning

2. make dinner
   making dinner

3. play basketball
   playing basketball

Listening Listen and circle the correct words.

"I study."	(every day)	right now
"I'm studying."	every day	(right now)

1.	(every day)	right now	5.	every day	right now
2.	every day	right now	6.	every day	right now
3.	every day	right now	7.	every day	right now
4.	every day	right now	8.	every day	right now

Grammar Circle the correct word.

1. Every day I (study studying).
2. Right now I'm (eat   eating).
3. Every day I (go   going) to school.
4. Right now I'm (do   doing) the laundry.
5. Every day I (make   making) breakfast.
6. Right now I'm (play   playing) the guitar.
7. Right now I'm (feed   feeding) the baby.
8. I (read   reading) every day.
9. I'm (iron   ironing) right now.
10. I'm (listen   listening) to music.

Grammar Circle the correct word.

| I clean the house. | I watch   TV. |
| My husband clean**s** the house. | My wife watch**es** TV. |

1. I (brush brushes) my teeth every day.
2. My son (clean   cleans) the house.
3. My sister (wash   washes) the dishes.
4. I (eat   eats) breakfast every day.
5. My brother (play   plays) the guitar.
6. My mother (exercise   exercises) every day.
7. I (go   goes) to work every day.
8. My father (cook   cooks) dinner every day.
9. I (comb   combs) my hair every day.
10. My grandson (watch   watches) TV every day.

A. **What's the weather?**

B. **It's sunny.**

Practice conversations with a partner.

A. What's the weather?

B. _____

1. It's cloudy.

2. It's hot.

3. It's cold.

4. It's raining.

5. It's snowing.

6. It's foggy.

What's the weather today where YOU live?

Listening  Listen and write the number under the correct picture.

___   ___   1   ___   ___

Weather Map

Practice conversations about the weather.

A. What's the weather today in _____?

(city)

B. It's _____.

(weather)

Community ⊙ Connections

Look in a newspaper. What's the weather today in different cities?

City	Weather	City	Weather

Practice conversations with these numbers.

A. How old are you?

B. I'm _____ years old.

A. What's your address?

B. _____ Main Street.

20	21	22	23	24
twenty	twenty-one	twenty-two	twenty-three	twenty-four
25	**26**	**27**	**28**	**29**
twenty-five	twenty-six	twenty-seven	twenty-eight	twenty-nine

30	40	50	60	70	80	90	100
thirty	forty	fifty	sixty	seventy	eighty	ninety	one hundred

Numbers Write the numbers.

thirty __30__   twenty-four _____   forty-one _____   eighty-two _____

fifty _____   twenty-six _____   sixty-seven _____   seventy-five _____

Temperatures

Look at the map on page 41 and practice conversations.

A. What's the temperature in _____?
(city)

B. It's _____ degrees.
(number)

Language Experience Journal

What do you do every day?
Write about it. Then read your
story to a classmate.

My Daily Life

Different Cultures   Different Ways

People in different families share household chores in different ways.

Who does the household chores in your home?
Who makes breakfast? Who makes lunch? Who makes dinner?
Who cleans? Who washes the dishes? Who does the laundry? Who irons?

PUT IT TOGETHER PART A

INFORMATION GAP ACTIVITY

Work with a partner. First, check (✓) the things
you do every day. Then ask each other:
What do you do every day? Compare your answers.

You		Your Partner
____	clean	____
____	wash the dishes	____
____	make dinner	____
____	iron	____
____	study	____
____	watch TV	____
____	listen to music	____
____	exercise	____

INFORMATION **GAP** ACTIVITY

Work with a partner. First, check (✓) the things you do every day. Then ask each other: What do you do every day? Compare your answers.

Do you clean the house every day?

{ Yes, I do. No, I don't.

You		Your Partner
_____	clean	_____
_____	wash the dishes	_____
_____	make dinner	_____
_____	iron	_____
_____	study	_____
_____	watch TV	_____
_____	listen to music	_____
_____	exercise	_____

VOCABULARY FOUNDATIONS

brush my teeth
clean
comb my hair
come home
cook dinner
do the laundry
eat breakfast/lunch/
    dinner
exercise
feed the baby
get dressed
get undressed
get up
go to bed
go to school
go to work
iron
listen to music
make breakfast/lunch/
    dinner

play basketball
play the guitar
read
study
take a shower
walk the dog
wash the dishes
watch TV

cloudy
cold
foggy
hot
raining
snowing
sunny
temperature

LANGUAGE SKILL FOUNDATIONS

I can . . .
☐ identify everyday activities
☐ ask about other people's everyday activities
☐ tell about my own everyday activities
☐ sequence everyday activities
☐ greet someone on the telephone
☐ tell someone what I'm doing
☐ describe the weather
☐ interpret a weather map
☐ find weather information in a newspaper
☐ use and write numbers 20–100

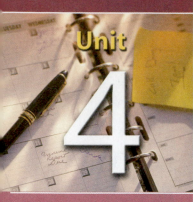

Numbers, Time, Calendar, Money

Vocabulary Preview

1 2 3 4 5 6 7 8 9 10

11 12 13 14 15 16 17 18 19 20

21 22 30 40 50 60 70 80 90 100

1 one	**11** eleven	**21** twenty-one
2 two	**12** twelve	**22** twenty-two
3 three	**13** thirteen	**30** thirty
4 four	**14** fourteen	**40** forty
5 five	**15** fifteen	**50** fifty
6 six	**16** sixteen	**60** sixty
7 seven	**17** seventeen	**70** seventy
8 eight	**18** eighteen	**80** eighty
9 nine	**19** nineteen	**90** ninety
10 ten	**20** twenty	**100** one hundred

Goals

- ► Cardinal numbers 1 – 100
- ► Time
- ► Days of the week
- ► Ordinal numbers
- ► Months of the year
- ► Coins and currency

	①	②	③	④	⑤	⑥	⑦
---	SUN	MON	TUE	WED	THU	FRI	SAT
				1	2	3	4	5
	6	7	8	9	10	11	12
	13	14	15	16	17	18	19
	20	21	22	23	24	25	26
	27	28	29	30	31		

⑧ JAN   ⑨ FEB   ⑩ MAR

⑪ APR   ⑫ MAY   ⑬ JUN

⑭ JUL   ⑮ AUG   ⑯ SEP

⑰ OCT   ⑱ NOV   ⑲ DEC

⑳   ㉑   ㉒   ㉓   ㉔   ㉕

1 Sunday	**8** January	**14** July	**20** penny
2 Monday	**9** February	**15** August	**21** nickel
3 Tuesday	**10** March	**16** September	**22** dime
4 Wednesday	**11** April	**17** October	**23** quarter
5 Thursday	**12** May	**18** November	**24** half dollar
6 Friday	**13** June	**19** December	**25** dollar bill
7 Saturday			

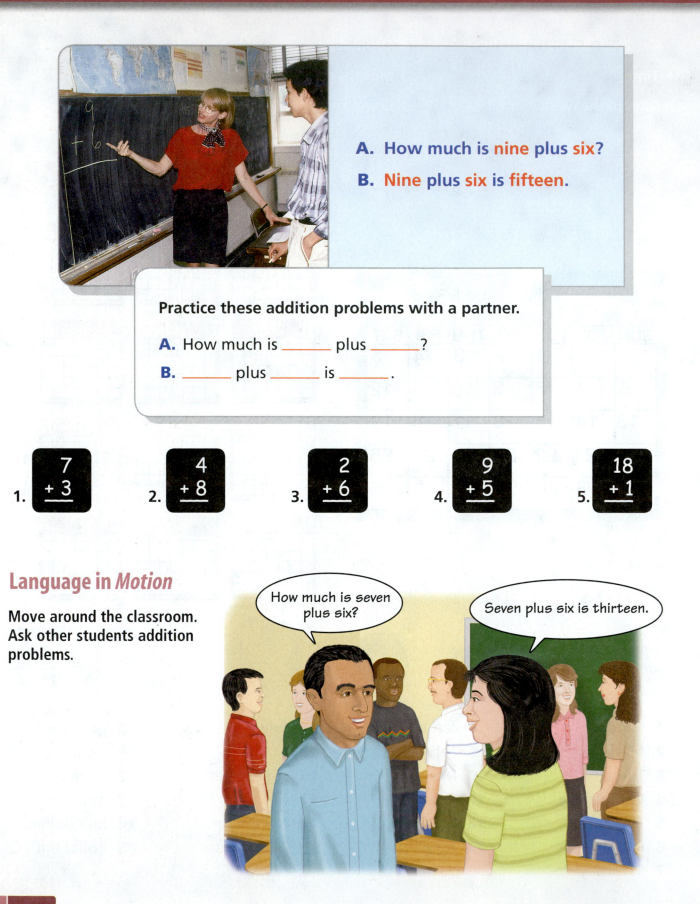

A. How much is nine plus six?

B. Nine plus six is fifteen.

Practice these addition problems with a partner.

A. How much is _____ plus _____?

B. _____ plus _____ is _____.

1.
```
  7
+ 3
```

2.
```
  4
+ 8
```

3.
```
  2
+ 6
```

4.
```
  9
+ 5
```

5.
```
 18
+ 1
```

Language in *Motion*

Move around the classroom. Ask other students addition problems.

How much is seven plus six?

Seven plus six is thirteen.

Pronunciation   Say the numbers.

1.	2	12	20
2.	3	13	30
3.	4	14	40
4.	5	15	50

5.	6	16	60
6.	7	17	70
7.	8	18	80
8.	9	19	90

Listening   Circle the number you hear.

1.	(8)	18
2.	12	20
3.	13	30
4.	14	40

5.	16	60
6.	7	70
7.	15	50
8.	19	90

Saying Large Address Numbers & Room Numbers

1422 Main Street	My address is **fourteen twenty-two** Main Street.
Room 317	My English class is in Room **three seventeen**.
Apartment 206	I am in Apartment **two oh six**.

1. 1749 Central Avenue	**5.** Room 219
2. 836 Main Street	**6.** Room 428
3. 5762 Washington Avenue	**7.** Apartment 311
4. 2308 Center Street	**8.** Apartment 504

Listening   Write the number you hear.

1. _14_	**5.** _____	**9.** _____
2. _____	**6.** _____	**10.** _____
3. _____	**7.** _____	**11.** _____
4. _____	**8.** _____	**12.** _____

It's one o'clock.

It's one fifteen.

It's one thirty.

It's one forty-five.

A. What time is it?

B. It's one o'clock.

Practice conversations with a partner.

A. What time is it?

B. It's _____ .

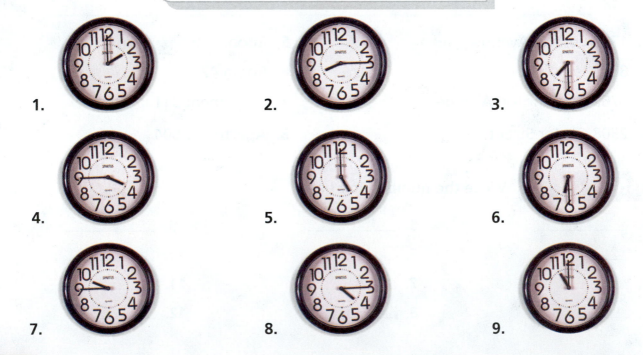

1.

2.

3.

4.

5.

6.

7.

8.

9.

Reading a Clock — Circle the correct time.

1. eleven o'clock   (ten o'clock)

2. eight thirty   eight forty-five

3. two fifteen   two thirty

4. nine o'clock   eleven forty-five

5. six o'clock   twelve o'clock

Listening  — Circle the time you hear.

1. (8:00)   8:30

2. 1:00   9:00

3. 7:00   11:00

4. 10:30   2:30

5. 4:00   4:30

6. 2:00   2:30

7. 3:15   3:45

8. 4:15   5:45

Writing Times

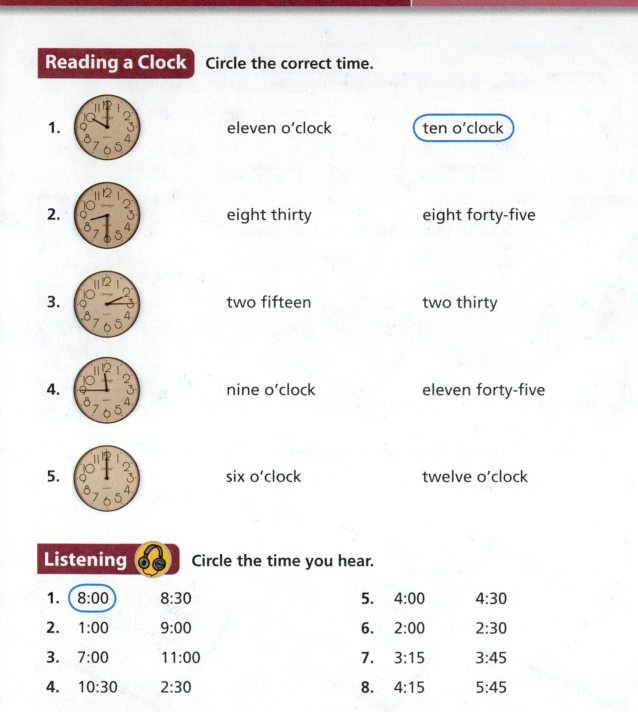

9:00   _____   _____   _____   _____

Sunday	Monday	Tuesday	Wednesday	Thursday	Friday	Saturday
1	**2**	**3**	**4**	**5**	**6**	

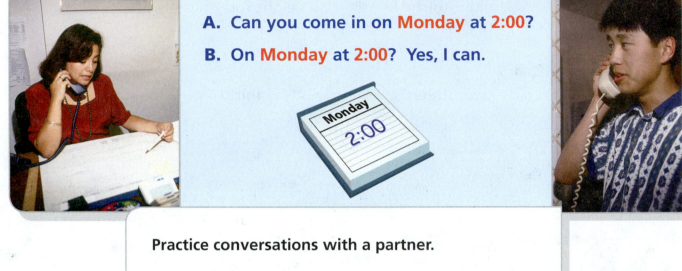

A. Can you come in on **Monday** at **2:00**?

B. On **Monday** at **2:00**? Yes, I can.

Monday
2:00

Practice conversations with a partner.

A. Can you come in on _____ at _____?

B. On _____ at _____? Yes, I can.

Tuesday
4:00

1.

Wednesday
1:15

2.

Thursday
10:30

3.

Friday
3:45

4.

Saturday
9:15

5.

Sunday
12:30

6.

Missing Days   Write the missing days.

1. Monday _____Tuesday_____ Wednesday
2. Wednesday _____ Friday
3. Friday _____ Sunday

4. Sunday _____ Tuesday
5. Tuesday _____ Thursday
6. Thursday _____ Saturday

Abbreviations   Write the days.

1. SUN _____Sunday_____
2. MON _____
3. TUE _____
4. WED _____
5. THU _____
6. FRI _____
7. SAT _____

SUN	MON	TUE	WED	THU	FRI	SAT
		1	2	3	4	5	6
7	8	9	10	11	12	13
14	15	16	17	18	19	20
21	22	23	24	25	26	27
28	29	30	31			

Listening 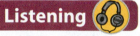   Circle the day you hear.

1. Tuesday   (Friday)
2. Sunday   Monday
3. Saturday   Wednesday
4. Thursday   Tuesday

5. SUN   SAT
6. MON   WED
7. FRI   SAT
8. THU   TUE

Listening    Write the time you hear on the correct day.

SUN	MON	TUE	WED	THU	FRI	SAT
			3:00			

53

1st	first
2nd	second
3rd	third
4th	fourth
5th	fifth
6th	sixth
7th	seventh
8th	eighth
9th	ninth
10th	tenth
11th	eleventh
12th	twelfth
13th	thirteenth
14th	fourteenth
15th	fifteenth
16th	sixteenth
17th	seventeenth
18th	eighteenth
19th	nineteenth
20th	twentieth
21st	twenty-first
22nd	twenty-second
30th	thirtieth
40th	fortieth
50th	fiftieth
60th	sixtieth
70th	seventieth
80th	eightieth
90th	ninetieth
100th	one hundredth

A. What floor do you live on?

B. I live on the third floor.

Practice conversations with a partner.

A. What floor do you live on?

B. I live on the _____ floor.

Matching

1.	seventh	16th		6.	fourteenth	40th
2.	sixteenth	20th		7.	fourth	14th
3.	second	2nd		8.	fortieth	44th
4.	sixtieth	7th		9.	forty-fourth	41st
5.	twentieth	60th		10.	forty-first	4th

Numbers   Write the numbers.

third	_3rd_	fifteenth	_____	sixteenth	_____	forty-second	_____
first	_____	fifth	_____	sixtieth	_____	twenty-ninth	_____
second	_____	fiftieth	_____	sixth	_____	eighty-first	_____
tenth	_____	fifty-fifth	_____	sixty-sixth	_____	thirty-third	_____

Listening 🎧   Circle the number you hear.

1.	7th	(17th)
2.	2nd	7th
3.	13th	30th
4.	5th	15th
5.	12th	20th
6.	1st	3rd
7.	21st	23rd
8.	14th	40th
9.	57th	67th
10.	92nd	97th
11.	35th	55th
12.	19th	90th

JANUARY	FEBRUARY	MARCH	APRIL	MAY	JUNE

JULY	AUGUST	SEPTEMBER	OCTOBER	NOVEMBER	DECEMBER

A. What month is it?

B. It's January.

A. Thanks.

Practice conversations with a partner.

A. What month is it?

B. It's _____.

A. Thanks.

A. What's the second month of the year?

B. February.

Practice conversations with a partner.

A. What's the _____ month of the year?

B. _____.

Abbreviations   Write the months.

JAN	_January_
FEB	_____
MAR	_____
APR	_____
MAY	_____
JUN	_____

JUL	_____
AUG	_____
SEP	_____
OCT	_____
NOV	_____
DEC	_____

How to Say a Date

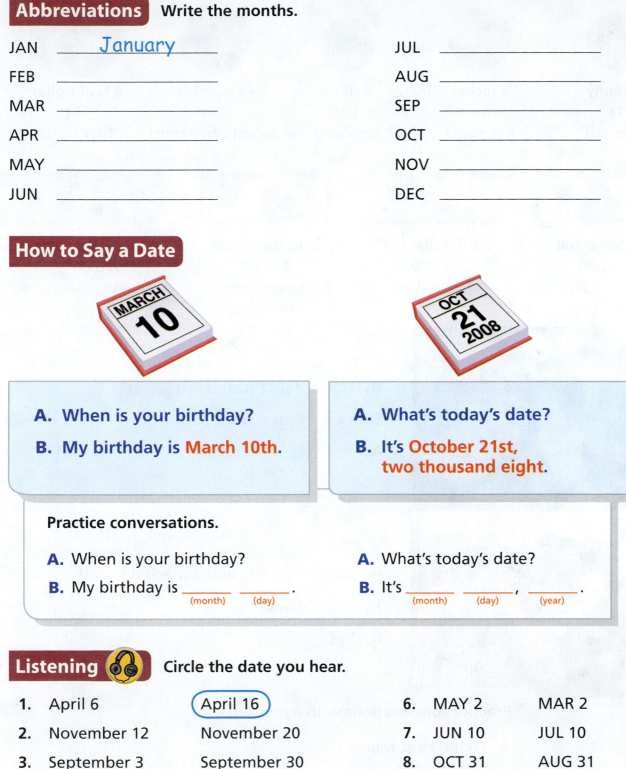

A. When is your birthday?

B. My birthday is March 10th.

A. What's today's date?

B. It's October 21st, two thousand eight.

Practice conversations.

A. When is your birthday?

B. My birthday is _____ _____.
    (month)   (day)

A. What's today's date?

B. It's _____ _____, _____.
    (month)   (day)   (year)

Listening   Circle the date you hear.

1.	April 6	(April 16)
2.	November 12	November 20
3.	September 3	September 30
4.	January 7	June 7
5.	August 21	October 21

6.	MAY 2	MAR 2
7.	JUN 10	JUL 10
8.	OCT 31	AUG 31
9.	SEP 3	NOV 1
10.	JAN 20	JUN 20

a penny
1¢
one cent

a nickel
5¢
five cents

a dime
10¢
ten cents

a quarter
25¢
twenty-five cents

a half dollar
50¢
fifty cents

a dollar bill
$1.00
one dollar

a 5-dollar bill
$5.00
five dollars

a 10-dollar bill
$10.00
ten dollars

a 20-dollar bill
$20.00
twenty dollars

A. Look! I just found **a quarter**!

B. **Twenty-five cents**?

A. Yes.

A. Look! I just found **a 10-dollar bill**!

B. **Ten dollars**?

A. Yes.

Practice conversations with a partner.

A. Look! I just found _____!

B. _____?

A. Yes.

Coin Values   Write the amount.

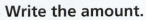

25¢   ____   ____   ____

Listening 🎧   Listen and write the number under the correct picture.

____   ____   ____

1   ____   ____

Listening 🎧   Circle the amount you hear.

1. (5¢) $5.00
2. 20¢ $20.00
3. 50¢ $50.00
4. $1.00   1¢

5. 35¢ $35.00
6. 10¢ $10.00
7. 75¢ $75.00
8. $1.00 $100.00

Language in *Motion*

Walk around the room. Ask other students addition problems with coins.

4 nickels   twenty cents   a dime and a quarter   thirty-five cents

Dates Write these important dates in your life.

My birthday _____

My favorite holiday _____

My _____'s birthday _____

My 1st day in this country _____

Community ▶◉ Connections

Write these days and times in your daily life.

	Days		Times	
I go to work	on _____	from _____	to _____.
I go to school	on _____	from _____	to _____.
I come home	on _____	at _____.

Memory Game

Walk around the room.
Ask students their birthdays.
Try to remember the dates.
Then say all the birthdays
you remember.

When is your birthday?

My birthday is April 10th.

Linda's birthday is April 10th. Mario's birthday is . . . .

Language Experience Journal

Write about your daily schedule.
When do you get up?
When do you eat breakfast?
When do you go to school or work?
When do you eat lunch?
When do you come home?
When do you eat dinner?
When do you go to bed?
Then read your story to a classmate.

My Daily Schedule

Different Cultures Different Ways

People in different cultures think of time in different ways.

In your culture, do people arrive on time for work?
Do people arrive on time for appointments?
Do people arrive on time for parties?
Tell about time in your culture.

PUT IT TOGETHER : PART A

INFORMATION GAP ACTIVITY

Work with a partner. You each have
different information about the same train
schedule. Ask each other about the following:

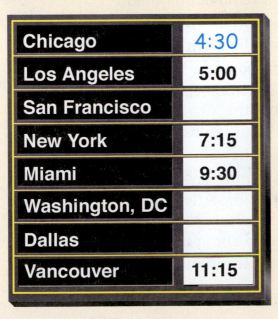

Chicago	4:30
Los Angeles	5:00
San Francisco	
New York	7:15
Miami	9:30
Washington, DC	
Dallas	
Vancouver	11:15

What time does the train to Chicago leave?

It leaves at 4:30.

INFORMATION GAP ACTIVITY

Work with a partner. You each have different information about the same train schedule. Ask each other about the following:

What time does the train to Chicago leave?

It leaves at 4:30.

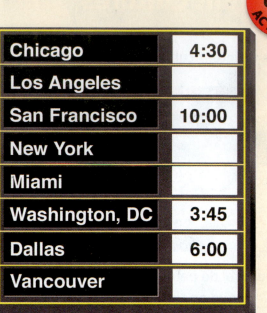

Chicago	4:30
Los Angeles	
San Francisco	10:00
New York	
Miami	
Washington, DC	3:45
Dallas	6:00
Vancouver	

VOCABULARY FOUNDATIONS

time	Sunday
o'clock	Monday
date	Tuesday
birthday	Wednesday
	Thursday
January	Friday
February	Saturday
March	
April	penny
May	nickel
June	dime
July	quarter
August	half dollar
September	dollar bill
October	
November	
December	

LANGUAGE SKILL FOUNDATIONS

I can . . .
- ☐ use cardinal numbers
- ☐ say addition problems
- ☐ ask and give the time
- ☐ say the days of the week
- ☐ make an appointment
- ☐ use ordinal numbers
- ☐ say the months of the year
- ☐ give dates
- ☐ read abbreviations for days and months
- ☐ identify coins and bills
- ☐ tell the value of coins and bills
- ☐ write money amounts
- ☐ give important days, times, and dates in my life
- ☐ write about my daily schedule
- ☐ talk about time in different cultures

Home

Vocabulary Preview

1 house
2 apartment building
3 bedroom

4 living room
5 kitchen
6 dining room

7 bathroom
8 balcony
9 patio

Goals

- ► **Rooms in the home**
- ► **Home appliances & features**
- ► **Types of housing**

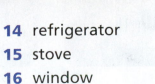

10 bathtub	**14** refrigerator	**18** bed	**22** table
11 shower	**15** stove	**19** chair	**23** lamp
12 closet	**16** window	**20** sofa	
13 cabinet	**17** fireplace	**21** rug	

A. **Tell me about the apartment.**

B. **It has a very nice living room.**

Practice conversations with a partner.

A. Tell me about the apartment.

B. It has a very nice _____.

1. kitchen

2. bedroom

3. bathroom

4. dining room

5. balcony

6. patio

Writing

1. The apartment has a nice _living room_.

2. The apartment has a small _____.

3. It also has a nice _____.

4. It also has a small _____.

5. There's a large _____.

6. There's a nice _____.

Listening 🎧 Listen and write the number under the correct picture.

_____   _____   _1_   _____   _____

Language in *Motion*

Walk around the room. Ask other students about where they live.

How many bedrooms are there where you live?

There are two bedrooms.

How many bathrooms are there?

There's one bathroom.

A. Is there a refrigerator in the kitchen?

B. Yes, there is.

Practice conversations with a partner.

A. Is there a _____ in the _____?

B. Yes, there is.

1. shower

bathroom

2. closet

bedroom

3. fireplace

living room

4. stove

kitchen

5. window

dining room

Listening

Listen and write the number under the correct picture.

_____   _____   _____   _1_   _____

Finish the Sentence

1. There's a shower in the _____.
2. There's a closet in the _____.
3. There's a stove in the _____.
4. There's a fireplace in the _____.

In Your Home   In your home, where do you . . .

cook? _____   watch TV? _____

eat? _____   take a bath? _____

Language in *Motion*

Pantomime an action at home. Other students guess the room you're in and the action.

A. Where do you want this **table**?

B. Put it in the **dining room**.

Practice conversations with a partner.

A. Where do you want this _____?

B. Put it in the _____.

1. sofa

2. bed

3. chair

4. rug

5. lamp

Memory Game

In my apartment, there's a table in the kitchen.

In my apartment, there's a table in the kitchen and a bed in the bedroom.

In my apartment, there's a table in the kitchen, a bed in the bedroom, and a rug in the dining room.

Stand in a circle. Repeat the things you hear. Add something new.

Community ▶ Connections

There are many different types of housing.

an apartment building

a house

a duplex

a mobile home

a dormitory

a shelter

What types of housing are there in your community?

Reading My Apartment

    I live in a nice apartment building on 12th Street. There are three floors in the building. I live on the second floor. There are six apartments in the building. I live in Apartment 4. There are four rooms in my apartment. There are three windows in the living room. There are two closets in the bedroom. There's a stove, there's a refrigerator, and there are four cabinets in the kitchen. The bathroom is also very nice. There's a shower, and there's a bathtub. This is my first apartment in this city, and I really like it!

1. How many floors are there in the building? _____ Three. _____

2. What street is the apartment building on? _____

3. How many apartments are there in the building? _____

4. Where is Apartment 4 in the building? _____

5. How many rooms are there in the apartment? _____

6. How many closets are there in the bedroom? _____

7. How many cabinets are there in the kitchen? _____

Language Experience Journal

Write about your home. Then read your story
to a classmate.

My Home

Different Cultures Different Ways

People around the world live in many different kinds of homes.

In your country, what kind of homes do people live in?
Describe a typical home.
How are these homes different from homes here?

PUT IT TOGETHER : PART A

INFORMATION GAP ACTIVITY

Work with a partner. You each have different
information about the same apartment. Ask
each other about the following:

refrigerator in the kitchen	_Yes_
shower in the bathroom	Yes
fireplace in the living room	No
stove in the kitchen	_____
closet in the bedroom	_____
window in the dining room	No

Is there a refrigerator in the kitchen?

Yes, there is.

PUT IT TOGETHER : PART B

INFORMATION GAP ACTIVITY

Work with a partner. You each have different information about the same apartment. Ask each other about the following:

refrigerator in the kitchen	Yes
shower in the bathroom	_____
fireplace in the living room	_____
stove in the kitchen	Yes
closet in the bedroom	No
window in the dining room	_____

Is there a refrigerator in the kitchen?

Yes, there is.

VOCABULARY FOUNDATIONS

balcony   bathtub
bathroom   bed
bedroom   cabinet
dining room   chair
kitchen   closet
living room   fireplace
patio   lamp
                 refrigerator
apartment building   rug
dormitory   shower
duplex   sofa
house   stove
mobile home   table
shelter   window

LANGUAGE SKILL FOUNDATIONS

I can . . .
☐ identify rooms in the home
☐ ask about an apartment
☐ ask about home appliances & features of an apartment
☐ describe activities in different rooms of a home
☐ identify furniture
☐ identify different types of housing in my community
☐ understand number information in a story
☐ compare different types of housing around the world

Talk About It! ▶ ▶ ▶ Where are these people? What are they doing?

75

Unit

6

Community

Vocabulary Preview

1 bakery	**4** clinic	**7** gas station
2 bank	**5** department store	**8** grocery store
3 bus station	**6** drug store	**9** hospital

76

Goals

▶ **Places in the community**

▶ **Asking for & giving location**

10 laundromat

11 library

12 movie theater

13 park

14 post office

15 restaurant

16 shopping mall

17 supermarket

18 train station

A. **Where are you going?**

B. **I'm going to the laundromat.**

Practice conversations with a partner.

A. Where are you going?

B. I'm going to the _____.

1. bank

2. clinic

3. bakery

4. library

5. gas station

6. bus station

7. drug store

8. grocery store

Listening

Listen and write the number under the correct picture.

_____ _____ _1_ _____ _____

Cloze Reading

Write the missing words.

Carlos is washing his clothes at the _____laundromat_____.¹ Monica is putting money in the _____.² Henry is reading a book in the _____.³ Jennifer is buying medicine in the _____.⁴ David is buying gas for his car at the _____.⁵

Missing Letters

1. c l i n i c
2. p __ r __
3. b a __ e __ y

4. __ a u n __ r o __ a t
5. d __ u g s __ o r __
6. __ u s s __ a t i o __

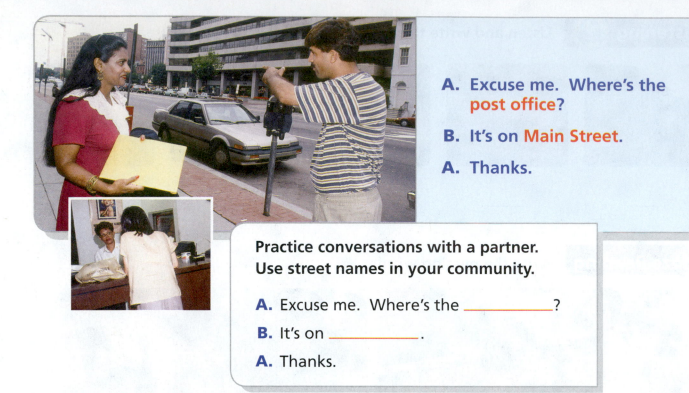

A. **Excuse me. Where's the post office?**

B. **It's on Main Street.**

A. **Thanks.**

Practice conversations with a partner. Use street names in your community.

A. Excuse me. Where's the _____?

B. It's on _____.

A. Thanks.

1. supermarket

2. hospital

3. park

4. restaurant

5. shopping mall

6. movie theater

7. train station

8. department store

Listening

Listen and write the number under the correct picture.

_____ __1__ _____ _____ _____

Cloze Reading   Write the missing words.

Wendy is buying stamps at the _____.¹ Tim is buying

food at the _____.² Hernan and Teresa are shopping at

the _____.³ Carl and Brenda are eating at a _____.⁴

Language in *Motion*

Pantomime an action in a place on pages 78–81. Other students guess the action and the place.

You're buying gas at a gas station!

You're eating at a restaurant!

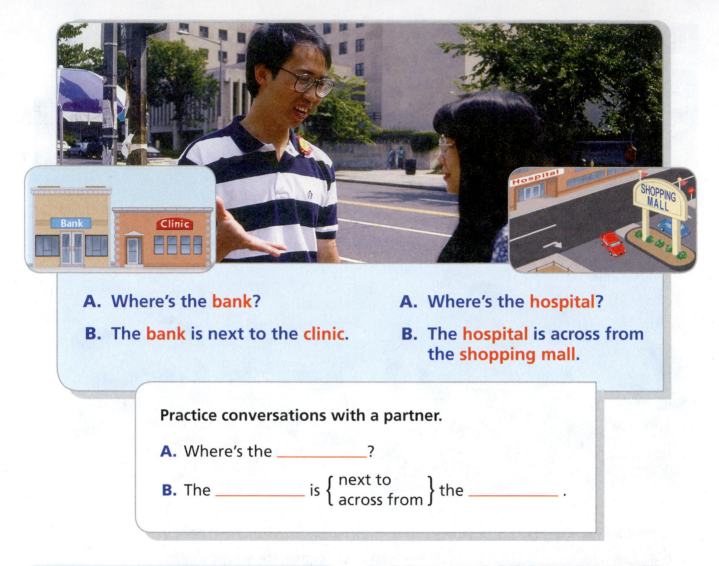

A. Where's the **bank**?

B. The **bank** is next to the **clinic**.

A. Where's the **hospital**?

B. The **hospital** is across from the **shopping mall**.

Practice conversations with a partner.

A. Where's the _____?

B. The _____ is { next to / across from } the _____ .

1. drug store

2. library

3. movie theater

4. restaurant

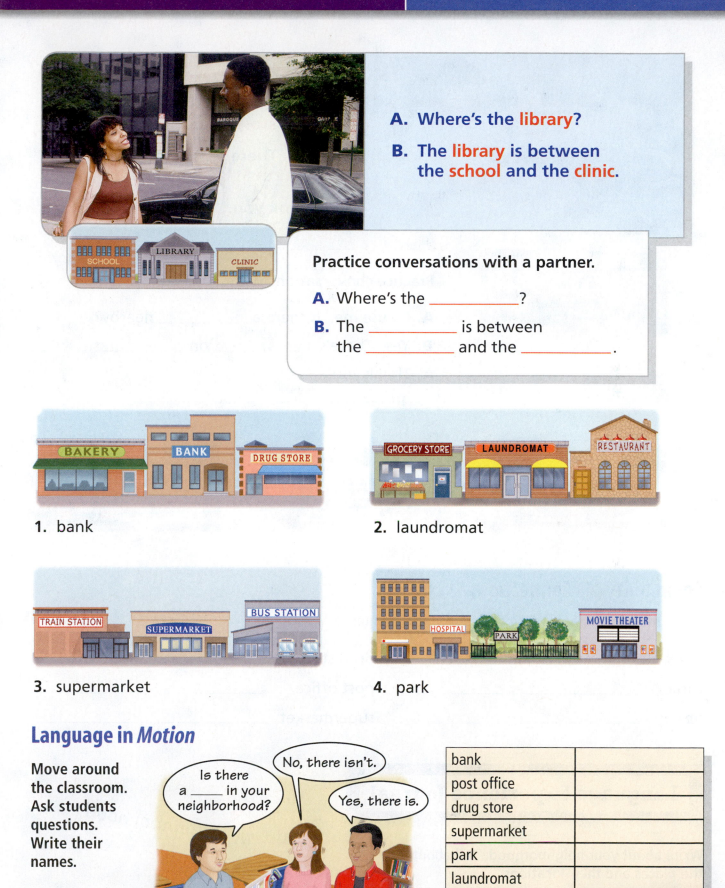

A. Where's the library?

B. The library is between the school and the clinic.

Practice conversations with a partner.

A. Where's the _____?

B. The _____ is between the _____ and the _____.

1. bank

2. laundromat

3. supermarket

4. park

Language in *Motion*

Move around the classroom. Ask students questions. Write their names.

Is there a _____ in your neighborhood?

No, there isn't.

Yes, there is.

bank	
post office	
drug store	
supermarket	
park	
laundromat	

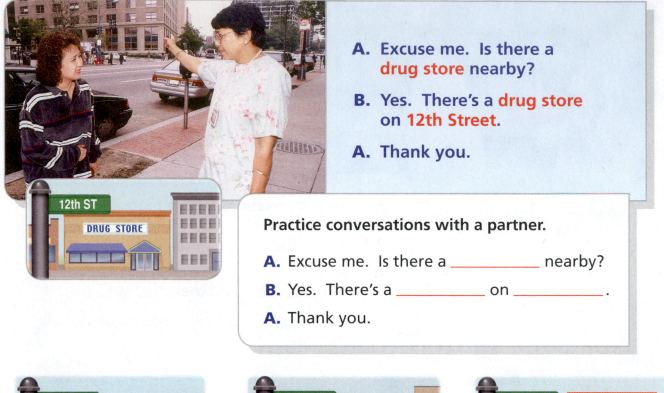

A. Excuse me. Is there a **drug store** nearby?

B. Yes. There's a **drug store** on **12th Street**.

A. Thank you.

Practice conversations with a partner.

A. Excuse me. Is there a _____ nearby?

B. Yes. There's a _____ on _____.

A. Thank you.

1.

2.

3.

Community ⊙ Connections

Write the addresses of these places in your community.

bank _____   drug store _____

clinic _____   post office _____

library _____   supermarket _____

Language Experience Journal

Write about your neighborhood. Tell about the places and their locations.

My Neighborhood

Different Cultures Different Ways

People in different communities shop in different places, such as large supermarkets, shopping malls, small stores, and markets.

Compare places people shop in different communities and countries.

PUT IT TOGETHER : PART A

INFORMATION GAP ACTIVITY

Work with a partner. You each have a map with different information. Ask each other questions and fill in the places on your maps.

What's across from the department store?

The gas station.

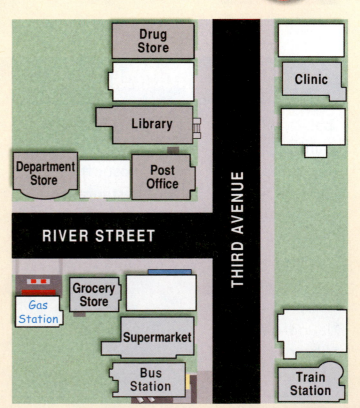

Drug Store

Clinic

Library

Department Store

Post Office

THIRD AVENUE

RIVER STREET

Gas Station

Grocery Store

Supermarket

Bus Station

Train Station

Work with a partner. You each have a map with different information. Ask each other questions and fill in the places on your maps.

What's across from the department store?

The gas station.

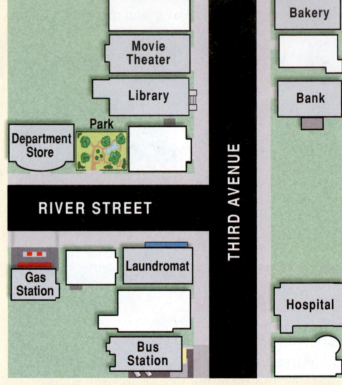

VOCABULARY FOUNDATIONS

bakery	movie theater
bank	park
bus station	post office
clinic	restaurant
department store	shopping mall
drug store	supermarket
gas station	train station
grocery store	
hospital	across from
laundromat	between
library	next to

LANGUAGE SKILL FOUNDATIONS

I can . . .

☐ identify places in the community
☐ ask for and give location of places
☐ identify street names
☐ tell about places in my neighborhood
☐ give the addresses of places in my community
☐ compare where people shop in different countries
☐ locate places on a map

Talk About It! ▶▶▶ **Where are these people? What are they saying?**

Describing

Vocabulary Preview

1

2

3

4

5

6

7

8

9

10

1 young	**4** tall	**7** single
2 middle-aged	**5** average height	**8** married
3 old	**6** short	**9** divorced
		10 widowed

Goals

- **Describing people:** Age, Height, Hair color, Eye color, Marital status
- **Describing feelings**

- **Countries & languages**
- **Titles**

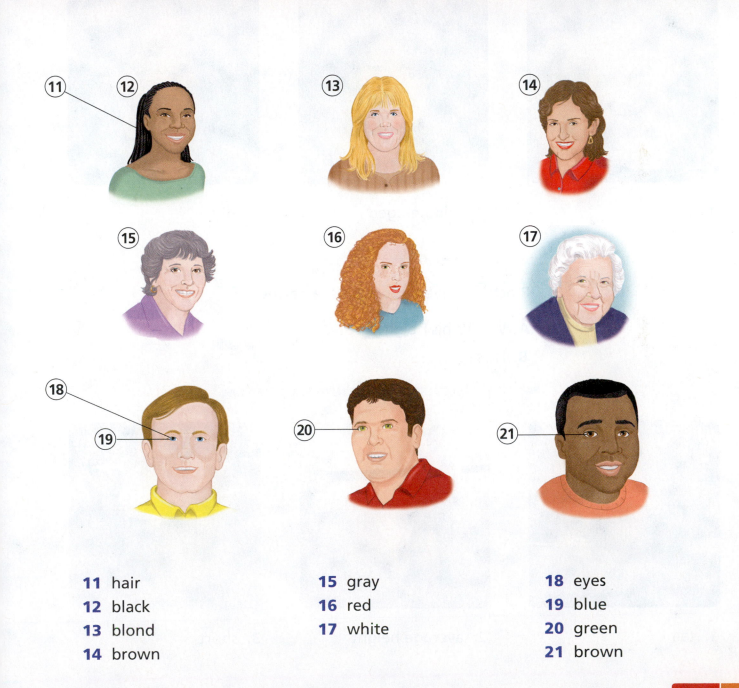

11 hair	**15** gray	**18** eyes
12 black	**16** red	**19** blue
13 blond	**17** white	**20** green
14 brown		**21** brown

89

Practice conversations with a partner.

A. What's her age?

B. She's _____.

1. young

2. middle-aged

3. old

Practice conversations with a partner.

A. What's his height?

B. He's _____.

1. tall

2. average height

3. short

Grammar   Rewrite the sentences.

I am	I'm
He is	He's
She is	She's
It is	It's
We are	We're
You are	You're
They are	They're

1. We are tall.   _We're tall._

2. She is young.   _____

3. I am short.   _____

4. They are old.   _____

5. He is middle-aged.   _____

6. You are average height. _____

Cloze Reading   Write the missing words.

average height   middle-aged   old   tall   young

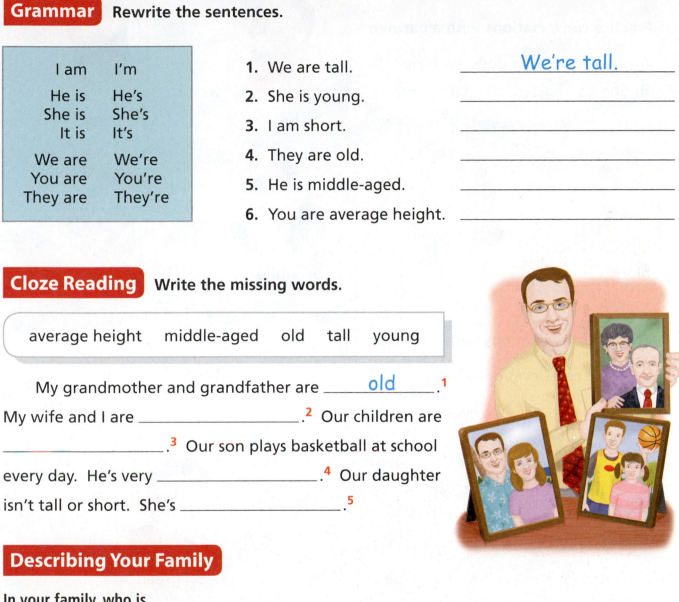

My grandmother and grandfather are _____old_____.[1]
My wife and I are _____.[2] Our children are
_____.[3] Our son plays basketball at school
every day. He's very _____.[4] Our daughter
isn't tall or short. She's _____.[5]

Describing Your Family

In your family, who is . . .

	Family Member	Name
young?		
middle-aged?		
old?		
tall?		
average height?		
short?		

Practice conversations with a partner.

A. What color hair does she have?

B. She has _____ hair.

1. brown

2. black

3. blond

4. red

5. white

6. gray

Practice conversations with a partner.

A. What color eyes does he have?

B. He has _____ eyes.

1. brown

2. blue

3. green

Grammar

I We You They	} have	He She It	} has

1. I ____have____ brown hair.

2. She _____ blue eyes.

3. He _____ gray hair.

4. Our children _____ black hair.

5. We _____ brown eyes.

6. I _____ blue eyes.

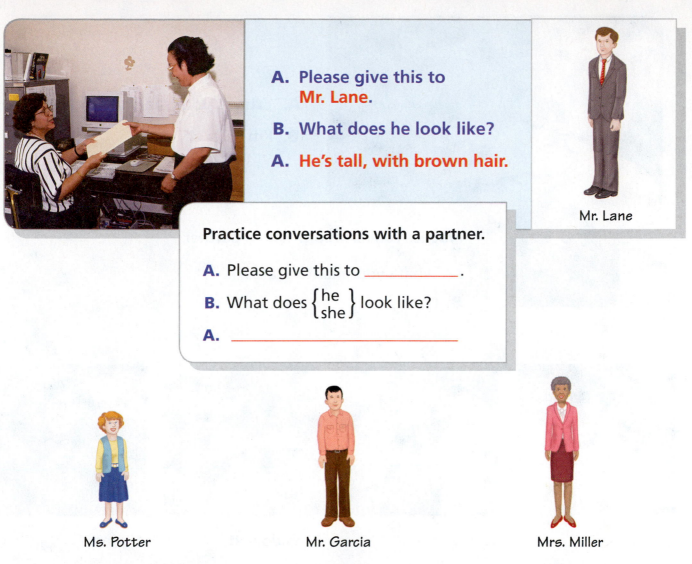

A. Please give this to Mr. Lane.

B. What does he look like?

A. He's tall, with brown hair.

Mr. Lane

Practice conversations with a partner.

A. Please give this to _____ .

B. What does { he / she } look like?

A. _____

Ms. Potter

Mr. Garcia

Mrs. Miller

1. She's short, with red hair.

2. He's average height, with black hair.

3. She's tall, with curly gray hair.

 **Listen and write the number next to the correct picture.**

 _____

 _____

 _____

 _____

 1

93

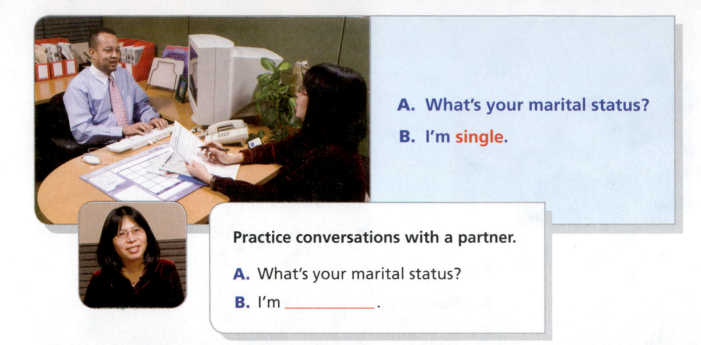

A. What's your marital status?

B. I'm single.

Practice conversations with a partner.

A. What's your marital status?

B. I'm _____.

1. married

2. divorced

3. widowed

4. single

Grammar

| I'm | He's | She's | We're | They're |

1. My brother isn't single. ___He's___ married.

2. My sister isn't married. _____ single.

3. Mr. and Mrs. Brown aren't married now. _____ divorced.

4. My husband and I aren't single. _____ married.

5. I'm not married now. _____ widowed.

Practice conversations with a partner.

A. Are you _____?

B. Yes. I'm very _____.

1. hungry

2. thirsty

3. happy

4. sad

5. tired

6. angry

7. sick

8. afraid

Finish the Sentence

1. When I'm hungry,   I go to bed.
2. When I'm tired,   I drink water.
3. When I'm thirsty,   I go to the clinic.
4. When I'm sick,   I eat.

Language in *Motion*

tired   sad

Pantomime a feeling.
Other students guess the word.

Describing People You Know

Fill in the chart about people in your family, in your English class, or other people you know.

Name	Age	Height	Hair Color	Eye Color	Marital Status
Tanya	middle-aged	short	black	brown	single

A. Where are you from?

B. I'm from Mexico.

A. What language do you speak?

B. I speak Spanish.

Practice conversations with a partner.

A. Where are you from?

B. I'm from _____ .

A. What language do you speak?

B. I speak _____ .

1. Korea
   Korean

2. Russia
   Russian

3. Haiti
   Haitian

4. Japan
   Japanese

5. China
   Chinese

6. Vietnam
   Vietnamese

7. Brazil
   Portuguese

8. Greece
   Greek

9. Morocco
   Arabic

Language in *Motion*

Move around the classroom. Ask six students. Write the information.

> What's your name?

> Where are you from?

> What language do you speak?

	Name	Country	Language
1.			
2.			
3.			
4.			
5.			
6.			

Fill Out the Form

(Please print)

NAME ⎸‿‿‿‿‿‿‿‿‿‿⎸ ⎸‿⎸ ⎸‿‿‿‿‿‿‿‿‿‿‿‿‿⎸
First   MI   Last

ADDRESS ⎸‿‿‿‿‿‿‿‿‿‿‿‿‿‿‿‿⎸
Number   Street

⎸‿‿‿‿‿‿‿‿‿‿‿‿⎸   ⎸‿‿⎸ ⎸‿‿‿‿⎸
City   State   Zip Code

COUNTRY OF ORIGIN _____   **LANGUAGE(S)** _____

(Circle)

HAIR COLOR: Black   Brown   Blond   Red   White   Gray

EYE COLOR: Brown   Blue   Black   Green   Other: _____

MARITAL STATUS: Single   Married   Divorced   Widowed

SIGNATURE _____   **TODAY'S DATE** ⎸‿‿‿⎸
                                                            Month Day Year

97

He's thin.

He's average weight.

He's heavy.

Match the sentences.

1. He weighs 70 pounds.   He's average weight.
2. He weighs 150 pounds.   He's heavy.
3. He weighs 210 pounds.   He's thin.

_____

1. He's 5 years old.   He's old.
2. He's 40 years old.   He's young.
3. He's 82 years old.   He's middle-aged.

_____

1. She's 5 feet tall.   She's tall.
2. She's 6 feet tall.   She's average height.
3. She's 5 feet 6 inches tall.   She's short.

Ways to Say It **Practice the questions and answers. Fill in the information.**

A. { What's your age?
     How old are you?

A. { What's your height?
     How tall are you?

A. { What's your weight?
     How much do you weigh?

B. I'm ____ years old.

B. I'm _____ tall.

B. I weigh _____.

Language Experience Journal

Write about yourself. Tell about your age, height, hair color, eye color, marital status, country, and languages.

About Me

Different Cultures Different Ways

People in different cultures show their feelings in different ways.

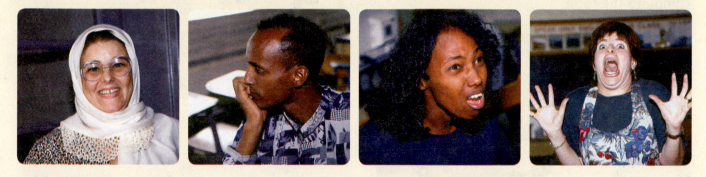

How are these people feeling?
In your culture, how do people show they're happy? sad? angry? afraid?

PUT IT TOGETHER : PART A

INFORMATION GAP ACTIVITY

Work with a partner. You each have different information. Ask each other questions and complete the form.

Name   Gloria   Robles
        First   Last
Address 74 Lake Street
        Number   Street
                        90017
        City   State   Zip Code
Telephone (213) 642-3197

Social Security Number _____

Country _____ Language Spanish

Hair Color Black   Eye Color _____

Marital Status _____

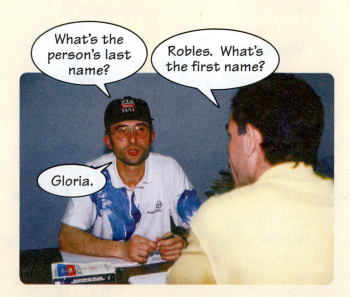

What's the person's last name?

Robles. What's the first name?

Gloria.

Work with a partner. You each have different information. Ask each other questions and complete the form.

What's the person's last name?

Robles. What's the first name?

Gloria.

Name   Gloria   Robles
        First   Last
Address _____
        Number   Street
        Los Angeles   CA   _____
        City   State Zip Code
Telephone _____
Social Security Number   074-38-9172
Country   Mexico   Language _____
Hair Color _____   Eye Color   Brown
Marital Status   Single _____

INFORMATION GAP ACTIVITY

VOCABULARY FOUNDATIONS

age
  young
  middle-aged
  old

height
  tall
  average height
  short

marital status
  single
  married
  divorced
  widowed

eyes
hair
country
language

black
blond
blue
brown
gray
green
red
white

afraid
angry
happy
hungry
sad
sick
thirsty
tired

LANGUAGE SKILL FOUNDATIONS

I can . . .
☐ describe people by age, height, hair color, eye color
☐ ask what people look like
☐ use titles (Mr., Ms., Mrs.)
☐ describe marital status
☐ ask about and express feelings
☐ identify native country and language
☐ fill out a personal information form
☐ compare how people show their feelings in different cultures

Food

Vocabulary Preview

1 apple	**5** carrot	**9** coffee	**13** hamburger
2 banana	**6** cereal	**10** cookie	**14** hot dog
3 bread	**7** cheese	**11** donut	**15** ice cream
4 butter	**8** cheeseburger	**12** egg	**16** lemonade

Goals

▶ **Common foods**

▶ **Expressing food needs**

▶ **Food containers & quantities**

▶ **Ordering food in a restaurant**

17 lettuce	21 orange	25 sandwich	29 taco
18 mayonnaise	22 peach	26 soda	30 tea
19 milk	23 pizza	27 soup	31 tomato
20 onion	24 potato	28 sugar	

A. **What are you looking for?**

B. **A cookie.**

A. **Sorry. There aren't any more cookies.**

Practice conversations with a partner.

A. What are you looking for?

B. _____.

A. Sorry. There aren't any more _____s.

1. a banana

2. a carrot

3. a tomato

4. a potato

5. a peach

6. an apple

7. an orange

8. an egg

9. an onion

Grammar   Circle the correct word.

a cookie	cookies
an apple	apples

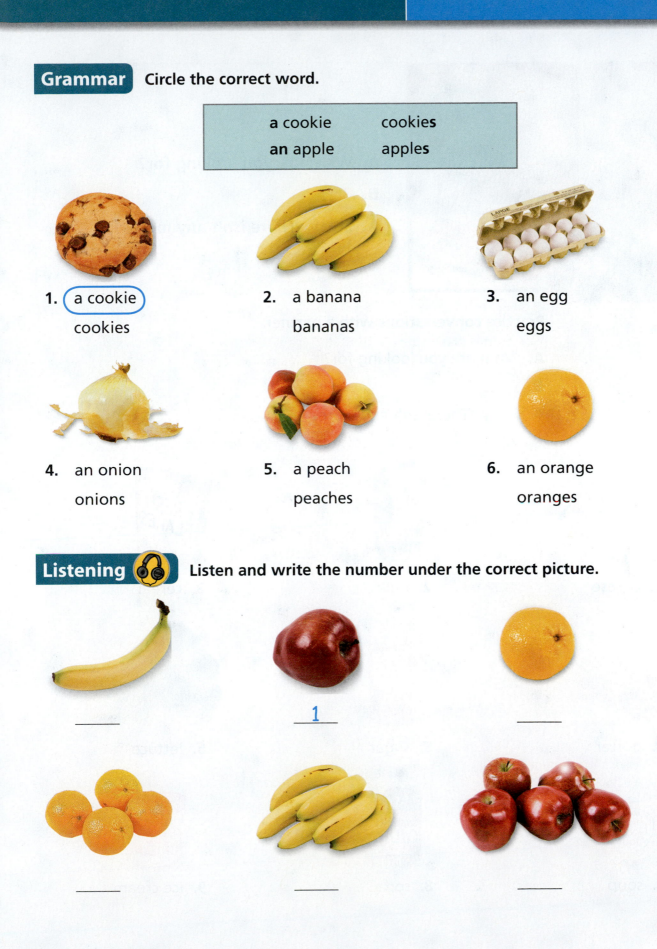

1. (a cookie)
   cookies

2. a banana
   bananas

3. an egg
   eggs

4. an onion
   onions

5. a peach
   peaches

6. an orange
   oranges

Listening   Listen and write the number under the correct picture.

_____

____1____

_____

_____

_____

_____

A. **What are you looking for?**

B. **Bread.**

A. **Sorry. There isn't any more bread.**

Practice conversations with a partner.

A. What are you looking for?

B. _____.

A. Sorry. There isn't any more _____.

1. cheese

2. milk

3. cereal

4. butter

5. sugar

6. lettuce

7. soup

8. soda

9. ice cream

Listening
Listen and write the number under the correct picture.

Grammar Write the correct word.

There **isn't** any more bread.
There **aren't** any more cookies.

1. There ___isn't___ any more soup.
2. There _____ any more bananas.
3. There _____ any more ice cream.
4. There _____ any more eggs.
5. There _____ any more carrots.
6. There _____ any more sugar.

Food in Your Home Tell about the food in your home today.

Yes, there is.   Yes, there are.
No, there isn't.   No, there aren't.

1. Is there any milk? _____
2. Are there any apples? _____
3. Is there any cereal? _____
4. Are there any eggs? _____
5. Are there any cookies? _____
6. Is there any cheese? _____

A. Excuse me.
   I'm looking for **bananas**.

B. **Bananas** are in Aisle 3.

A. Thank you.

Practice conversations with a partner.

A. Excuse me. I'm looking for _____.

B. _____ are in Aisle 3.

A. Thank you.

1.   2.   3.

A. Excuse me.
   I'm looking for **milk**.

B. **Milk** is in Aisle 1.

A. Thank you.

Practice conversations with a partner.

A. Excuse me. I'm looking for _____.

B. _____ is in Aisle 1.

A. Thank you.

1.   2.   3.

Grammar Write the correct word.

is	are

1. Onions __are__ in Aisle 4.
2. Sugar _____ in Aisle 3.
3. Eggs _____ in Aisle 7.

4. Tomatoes _____ in Aisle 2.
5. Lettuce _____ in Aisle 6.
6. Soda _____ in Aisle 1.

Categories Write the words in the correct section.

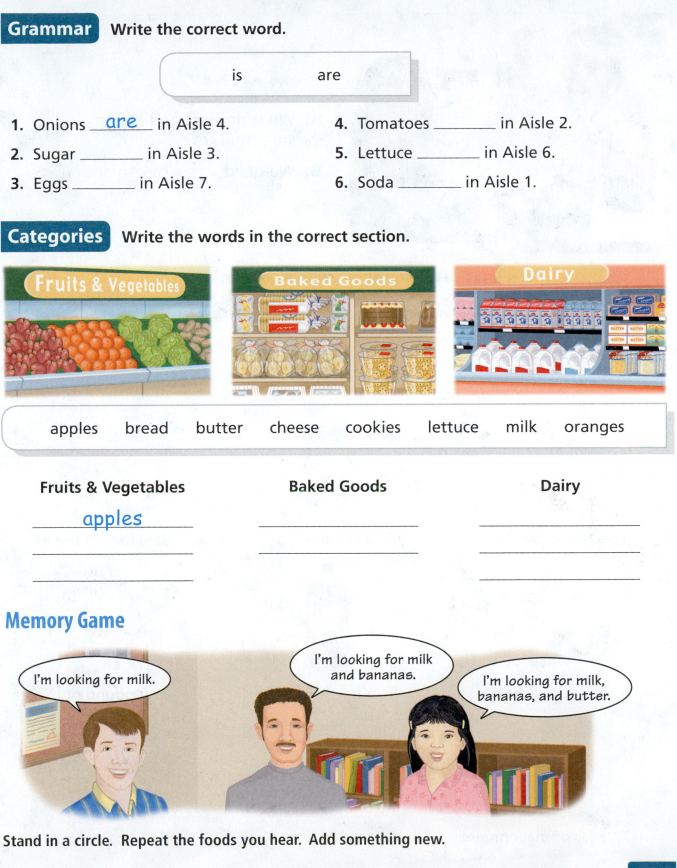

Fruits & Vegetables   Baked Goods   Dairy

apples   bread   butter   cheese   cookies   lettuce   milk   oranges

Fruits & Vegetables

_____apples_____

_____

_____

Baked Goods

_____

_____

_____

Dairy

_____

_____

_____

Memory Game

I'm looking for milk.

I'm looking for milk and bananas.

I'm looking for milk, bananas, and butter.

Stand in a circle. Repeat the foods you hear. Add something new.

A. What do we need at the supermarket?

B. We need **a box of cookies.**

Practice conversations with a partner.

A. What do we need at the supermarket?

B. We need _____.

1. a bag of sugar

2. a can of soup

3. a loaf of bread

4. a bunch of bananas

5. a bottle of soda

6. a pound of cheese

7. a jar of mayonnaise

8. a quart of milk

9. a dozen eggs

Matching

1. bottle  sugar
2. bag cheese
3. dozen soda
4. jar eggs
5. pound mayonnaise

6. loaf milk
7. box bread
8. can soup
9. quart bananas
10. bunch cookies

Listening

Listen and write the number under the correct picture.

Memory Game

Stand in a circle. Repeat the foods you hear. Add something new.

A. Can I help you?

B. Yes. I'd like **a hamburger**, please.

Practice conversations with a partner.

A. Can I help you?

B. Yes. I'd like _____, please.

1. a hot dog

2. a sandwich

3. a cheeseburger

4. a taco

5. a pizza

6. a donut

7. lemonade

8. coffee

9. tea

Listening

Listen and write the number under the correct picture.

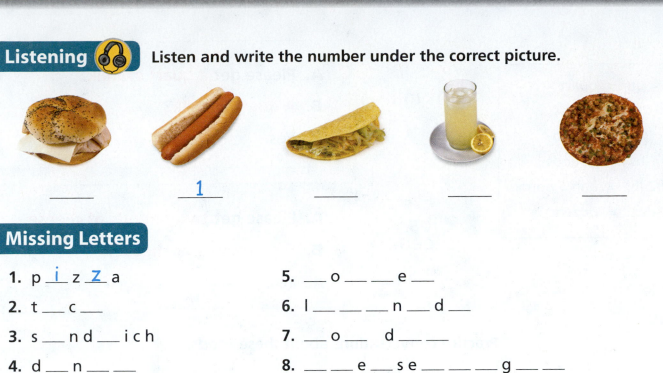

____   __1__   ____   ____   ____

Missing Letters

1. p _i_ z _z_ a
2. t __ c __
3. s __ n d __ i c h
4. d __ n __ __

5. __ o __ __ e __
6. l __ __ __ n __ d __
7. __ o __ d __ __
8. __ __ e __ s e __ __ __ g __ __

Community ▶ Connections

What food stores do you go to?
What do you buy there? Make a list,
and discuss with other students.

Store	Foods

Do you go to fast-food restaurants? Where do you go? What foods do you like there?
Make a list, and discuss with other students.

Fast-Food Restaurant	Foods

qt. = quart
qts. = quarts
lb. = pound
lbs. = pounds
1/2 lb. = half a pound
doz. = dozen

1 qt. milk

A. Please get a quart of milk.

B. A quart of milk?

A. Yes.

2 lbs. cheese

A. Please get two pounds of cheese.

B. Two pounds of cheese?

A. Yes.

Practice conversations about these foods.

A. Please get _____.

B. _____?

A. Yes.

1 lb. cheese

2 qts. milk

1 doz. eggs

1. a pound of cheese **2.** two quarts of milk **3.** a dozen eggs

3 lbs. apples

1/2 lb. tomatoes

1/2 doz. oranges

4. three pounds of apples **5.** half a pound of tomatoes **6.** half a dozen oranges

Make a shopping list on a piece of paper. Compare lists with another student.

Language Experience Journal

My Favorite Food

What's your favorite food? Why do you like it? When do you eat it? Write about it.

Different Cultures   Different Ways

People around the world eat many different kinds of foods.

Tell about foods in your culture.
What do people eat for breakfast? lunch? dinner?

PUT IT TOGETHER PART A

INFORMATION GAP ACTIVITY

**Work with a partner. What foods do you have
in your kitchens? Ask each other about this list
of foods.**

	You	Your Partner
milk	No	Yes
cookies	Yes	No
soda	No	____
eggs	No	____
ice cream	Yes	____
oranges	Yes	____
butter	No	____
carrots	No	____

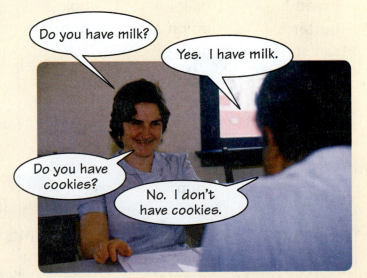

PUT IT TOGETHER PART B

Work with a partner. What foods do you have in your kitchens? Ask each other about this list of foods.

	You	Your Partner
milk	**Yes**	_____
cookies	**No**	_____
soda	**No**	_____
eggs	**Yes**	_____
ice cream	**Yes**	_____
oranges	**No**	_____
butter	**Yes**	_____
carrots	**No**	_____

VOCABULARY FOUNDATIONS

apple	lettuce	bag
banana	mayonnaise	bottle
bread	milk	box
butter	onion	bunch
carrot	orange	can
cereal	peach	dozen
cheese	pizza	jar
cheeseburger	potato	loaf
coffee	sandwich	pound
cookie	soda	quart
donut	soup	
egg	sugar	
hamburger	taco	
hot dog	tea	
ice cream	tomato	
lemonade		

LANGUAGE SKILL FOUNDATIONS

I can . . .
- ☐ name common foods
- ☐ express food needs
- ☐ identify food categories
- ☐ identify food containers and quantities
- ☐ name common restaurant foods
- ☐ order food in a restaurant
- ☐ recommend food stores and restaurants in my community
- ☐ make a shopping list
- ☐ tell about my favorite food
- ☐ compare foods and meals in different cultures

Talk About It! ▶▶▶ What foods are these people buying at the supermarket?

117

Unit 9

Clothing, Colors, & Shopping

Vocabulary Preview

1 belt	5 gloves	9 necklace	
2 blouse	6 jacket	10 pajamas	
3 coat	7 jeans	11 pants	
4 dress	8 mittens	12 shirt	

Goals

▶ **Clothing items**

▶ **Asking for clothing in a store**

▶ **Colors**

▶ **Clothing sizes**

▶ **Problems with clothing**

▶ **Prices**

13 shoes	**17** sweater	**21** small
14 skirt	**18** tie	**22** medium
15 socks	**19** umbrella	**23** large
16 suit	**20** watch	**24** extra-large

A. I'm looking for a shirt.

B. Shirts are over there.

A. Thank you.

Practice conversations with a partner.

A. I'm looking for _____ .

B. _____s are over there.

A. Thank you.

1. a coat

2. a suit

3. a belt

4. a jacket

5. a tie

6. a sweater

7. an umbrella

8. a blouse

9. a dress

10. a watch

11. a necklace

Listening  Listen and write the number under the correct picture.

_____   _____   _____   1   _____

One or More? Circle the correct word.

1. tie
   (ties)

2. blouse
   blouses

3. skirt
   skirts

4. umbrella
   umbrellas

5. sweater
   sweaters

6. necklace
   necklaces

Pronunciation Write and say the words.

a coat	coats	a sweater	sweaters	a dress	dresses
a shirt	_____	a tie	_____	a watch	_____
a suit	_____	an umbrella	_____	a blouse	_____

Grammar Circle the correct word.

1. I'm looking for a ((dress) dresses).
2. (Belt   Belts) are over there.
3. I'm looking for a (watch   watches).
4. (Suit   Suits) are over there.
5. Where are (jacket   jackets)?
6. I'm looking for a (tie   ties).
7. (Blouse   Blouses) are over there.
8. Where are (coat   coats)?

A. May I help you?

B. Yes. I'm looking for a pair of **shoes**.

A. **Shoes** are over there.

Practice conversations with a partner.

A. May I help you?

B. Yes. I'm looking for a pair of _____.

A. _____ are over there.

1. pants

2. socks

3. jeans

4. gloves

5. mittens

6. pajamas

Listening  Listen and write the number under the correct picture.

___ ___1___ ___ ___

___ ___ ___ ___

Missing Letters

1. s _o_ c k _s_
2. j __ __ n s
3. p __ n t __

4. __ i __ __ e n s
5. __ __ o e __
6. __ a __ a __ a __

Memory Game

I'm looking for a jacket.

I'm looking for a jacket and a pair of socks.

I'm looking for a jacket, a pair of socks, and an umbrella.

Stand in a circle. Repeat the clothing you hear. Add something new.

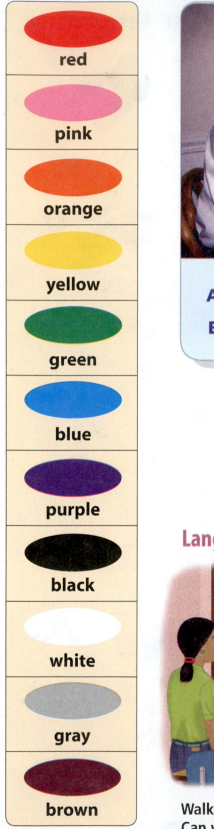

red

pink

orange

yellow

green

blue

purple

black

white

gray

brown

A. **What's your favorite color?**

B. **Blue.**

Practice conversations with a partner.

A. What's your favorite color?

B. _____ .

Language in *Motion*

What's your favorite color?

**Walk around the room. Ask other students.
Can you remember their favorite colors?**

What Are They Wearing?

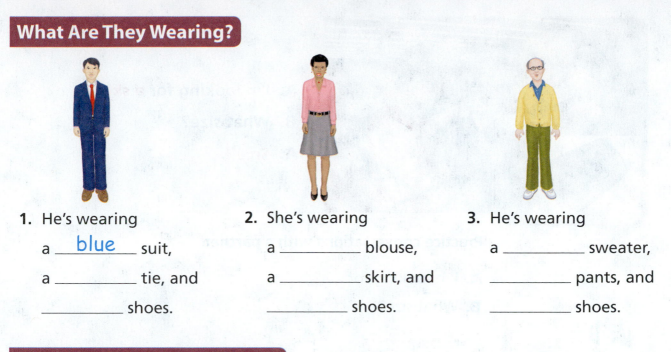

1. He's wearing
   a __blue__ suit,
   a _____ tie, and
   _____ shoes.

2. She's wearing
   a _____ blouse,
   a _____ skirt, and
   _____ shoes.

3. He's wearing
   a _____ sweater,
   _____ pants, and
   _____ shoes.

What Are You Wearing Today?

Practice conversations with other students.

A. What are you wearing today?

B. I'm wearing _____ _____, _____ _____,
(color)   (clothing)   (color)   (clothing)

and _____ _____.
(color)   (clothing)

Guessing Game

Describe the clothing of another student. Your classmates guess the student's name.

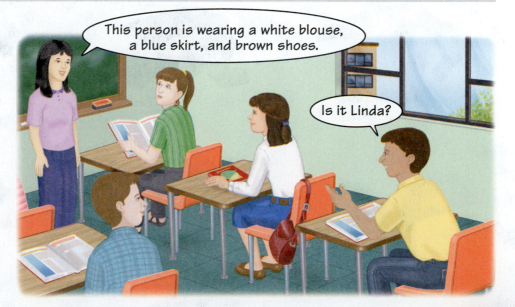

This person is wearing a white blouse, a blue skirt, and brown shoes.

Is it Linda?

A. I'm looking for **a skirt**.

B. **What size?**

A. **Small.**

Practice conversations with a partner.

A. I'm looking for _____.

B. What size?

A. _____.

1. medium

2. large

3. size 36

4. size 15

5. size 40

6. size 12

7. size 34

8. size 10

9. size 32

What Size Do You Wear?   Practice conversations with other students.

A. What size _____ do you wear?
   (clothing)

B. _____ .
   (size)

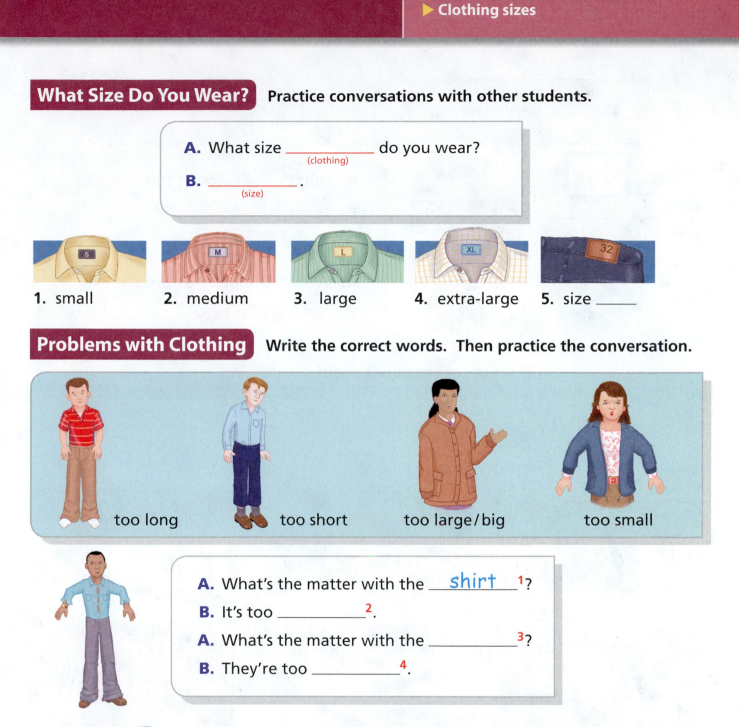

1. small
2. medium
3. large
4. extra-large
5. size _____

Problems with Clothing   Write the correct words. Then practice the conversation.

too long   too short   too large / big   too small

A. What's the matter with the ___*shirt*___ ¹?

B. It's too _____ ².

A. What's the matter with the _____ ³?

B. They're too _____ ⁴.

Community ▶ Connections

Where do you shop for different types of clothing? What stores do you go to?
Where are they? Make a list and discuss with other students.

Clothing	Store	Location

$10.00 = ten dollars

$10.50 = { ten dollars and fifty cents
ten fifty

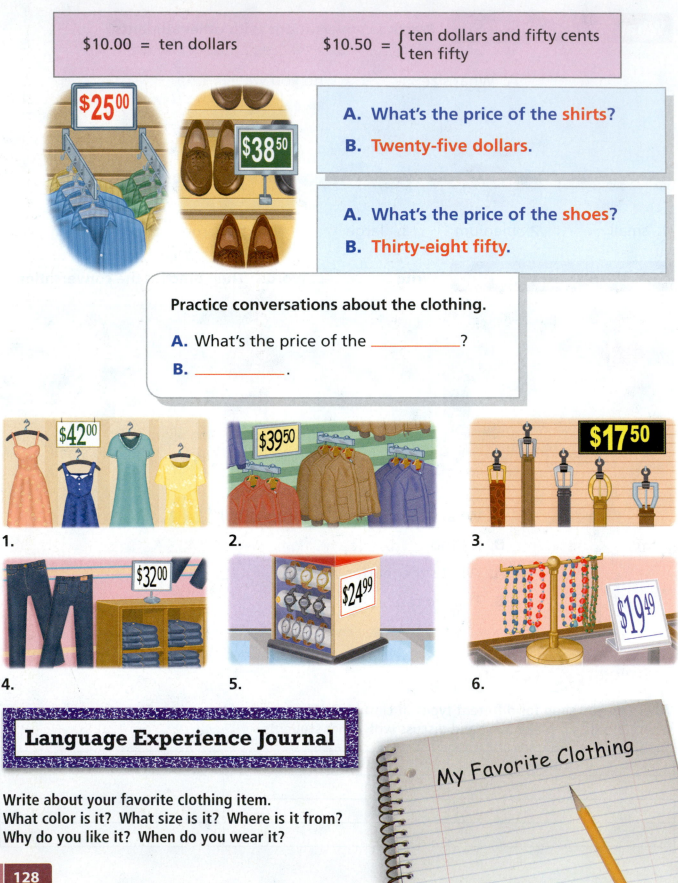

$25⁰⁰

$38⁵⁰

A. What's the price of the **shirts**?
B. Twenty-five dollars.

A. What's the price of the **shoes**?
B. Thirty-eight fifty.

Practice conversations about the clothing.

A. What's the price of the _____?
B. _____.

$42⁰⁰

$39⁵⁰

$17⁵⁰

1.

2.

3.

$32⁰⁰

$24⁹⁹

$19⁴⁹

4.

5.

6.

Language Experience Journal

Write about your favorite clothing item.
What color is it? What size is it? Where is it from?
Why do you like it? When do you wear it?

My Favorite Clothing

Different Cultures   *Different Ways*

People in different cultures have special clothing for special days.

What special day do you think it is?
What special clothing do people in your country wear?
When do they wear this clothing?

PUT IT TOGETHER : PART **A**

INFORMATION GAP ACTIVITY

Work with a partner. You each have different information about the same store. Ask each other about these clothing items.

SHOES	1
COATS	3
MEN'S SHIRTS	___
WOMEN'S BLOUSES	4
WATCHES	I
TIES	___
UMBRELLAS	___
NECKLACES	I

Where are shoes?

Shoes are on the first floor.

Work with a partner. You each have different information about the same store. Ask each other about these clothing items.

Where are shoes?

Shoes are on the first floor.

SHOES	1
COATS	___
MEN'S SHIRTS	2
WOMEN'S BLOUSES	___
WATCHES	___
TIES	2
UMBRELLAS	5
NECKLACES	___

VOCABULARY FOUNDATIONS

belt	sweater	size
blouse	tie	small
coat	umbrella	medium
dress	watch	large
gloves		extra-large
jacket	black	
jeans	blue	too long
mittens	brown	too short
necklace	gray	too large / too big
pajamas	green	
pants	orange	too small
shirt	pink	
shoes	purple	price
skirt	red	
socks	white	a pair of
suit	yellow	

LANGUAGE SKILL FOUNDATIONS

I can . . .
- ☐ identify clothing items
- ☐ ask for clothing in a store
- ☐ name colors
- ☐ tell about my favorite color
- ☐ describe what people are wearing
- ☐ identify clothing sizes
- ☐ describe problems with clothing
- ☐ list clothing stores in my community
- ☐ identify prices of clothing
- ☐ tell about my favorite clothing
- ☐ tell about special clothing in different cultures
- ☐ locate items using a store directory

On Sale $37.50

$19.99

$4.99

$29.99

$32.50

SALE

Talk About It! ▶▶▶ **What clothing are these people looking for?**

Vocabulary Preview

1 bank	**4** deposit slip	**6** check
2 bank book	**5** withdrawal slip	**7** checkbook
3 ATM card		**8** credit card

Goals

- ► Bank items
- ► Checks
- ► Making change
- ► Postal items
- ► Obtaining post office services

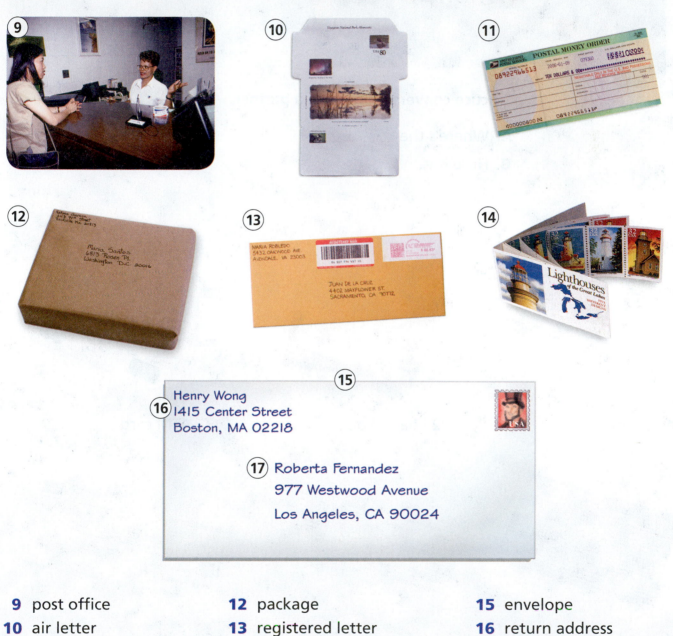

9 post office	**12** package	**15** envelope
10 air letter	**13** registered letter	**16** return address
11 money order	**14** stamps	**17** mailing address

Henry Wong
1415 Center Street
Boston, MA 02218

Roberta Fernandez
977 Westwood Avenue
Los Angeles, CA 90024

A. Where's the **checkbook**?

B. Here it is.

Practice conversations with a partner.

A. Where's the _____?

B. Here it is.

1. check

2. bank book

3. ATM card

4. credit card

5. deposit slip

6. withdrawal slip

Listening  Listen and write the number under the correct picture.

_____   _____    1

_____   _____   _____

Matching

1. When I write a check, I use my   deposit slip.

2. When I put money in the bank, I use a   credit card.

3. When I charge items in a store, I use my   ATM card.

4. When I take money out of the bank, I use a   checkbook.

5. When I use a machine at the bank, I use my   withdrawal slip.

Community Connections

Ask four students. Write the information on the chart.

Do you have a bank account?

What is the name of your bank?

Do you have. . . a checkbook? an ATM card? a credit card?

Student's Name	Name of Bank	Checkbook?	ATM card?	Credit card?
_____	_____	☐	☐	☐
_____	_____	☐	☐	☐
_____	_____	☐	☐	☐
_____	_____	☐	☐	☐

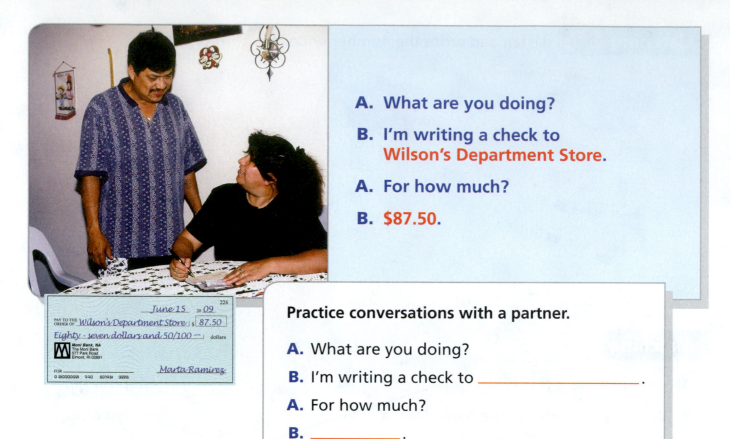

A. **What are you doing?**

B. **I'm writing a check to Wilson's Department Store.**

A. **For how much?**

B. **$87.50.**

Practice conversations with a partner.

A. What are you doing?

B. I'm writing a check to _____.

A. For how much?

B. _____.

1.

2.

3.

4.

Writing Checks

Complete these checks. Write today's date, the dollar amount in numbers and words, and sign your name.

1. $22.40

250

June 15 20 09

PAY TO THE ORDER OF _Express Cleaners_ $ 22.40

Twenty-two and 40/100——————— dollars

Moni Bank, NA
The Moni Bank
577 Park Road
Elmont, RI 02891

FOR _shirts and pants_   _Vicki Chen_

⑈ 2⑈0000021 990 507991 0250

2. $87.50

251

20 ___

PAY TO THE ORDER OF _Dr. Crawford_ $

dollars

Moni Bank, NA
The Moni Bank
577 Park Road
Elmont, RI 02891

FOR _office visit_

⑈ 2⑈0000021 990 507991 0251

3. $43.92

252

20 ___

PAY TO THE ORDER OF _Southwest Electric_ $

dollars

Moni Bank, NA
The Moni Bank
577 Park Road
Elmont, RI 02891

FOR _electric bill_

⑈ 2⑈0000021 990 507991 0252

4. $113.58

253

20 ___

PAY TO THE ORDER OF _Worldcard_ $

dollars

Moni Bank, NA
The Moni Bank
577 Park Road
Elmont, RI 02891

FOR _credit card bill_

⑈ 2⑈0000021 990 507991 0253

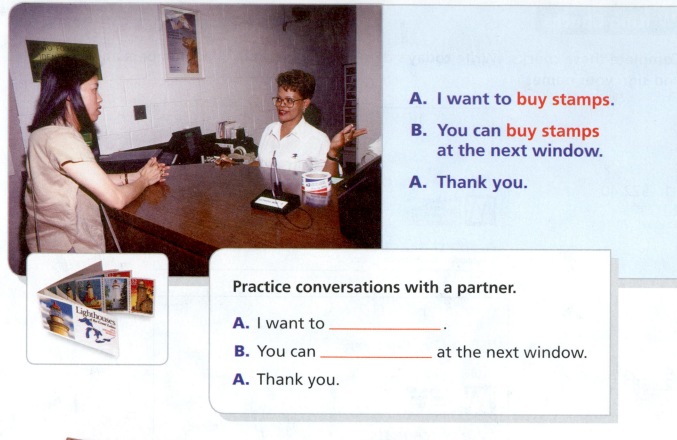

A. I want to **buy stamps.**

B. You can **buy stamps** at the next window.

A. Thank you.

Practice conversations with a partner.

A. I want to _____ .

B. You can _____ at the next window.

A. Thank you.

1. mail a package

2. send a registered letter

3. buy a money order

4. buy an air letter

Matching

Look at the post office windows. Write the correct number under each picture.

| 1 STAMPS | 2 PACKAGES | 3 REGISTERED MAIL | 4 MONEY ORDERS | 5 AIR LETTERS |

2 ___   ___   ___   ___   ___

An Envelope

Henry Wong
1415 Center Street
Boston, MA 02218

Roberta Fernandez
977 Westwood Avenue
Los Angeles, CA 90024

Who is this letter going to? _____

What's the mailing address? _____

Who is this letter from? _____

What's the return address? _____

Community Connections

Go to your local post office. What days is the post office open?
What time does it open? What time does it close? Fill in the chart.

	SUN	MON	TUE	WED	THU	FRI	SAT
Open							
Close							

$20.00
−17.50
$ 2.50

$17.50

A. That's **$17.50**.

B. Here's **$20.00**.

A. Your change is **$2.50**.

Practice conversations with a partner.

A. That's _____.

B. Here's _____.

A. Your change is _____.

$36.00

$8.50

$8.50

$3.20

1. $40.00
    − 36.00

2. $10.00
    − 8.50

3. $5.00
    − 3.20

$42.40

$94.80

$94.80

$56.90

4. $50.00
    − 42.40

5. $100.00
    − 94.80

6. $60.00
    − 56.90

Language Experience Journal

Saving Money

How do you save money? Do you buy things on
sale? Do you shop at discount stores? Do you go
to yard sales? Write about it.

Different Cultures   Different Ways

Different countries have different coins and bills.

What are the names of
coins and bills in your
country? What are
their values?
What coins and bills
from other countries do
you know?

PUT IT TOGETHER : PART A

INFORMATION GAP ACTIVITY

Work with a partner. You each have different information about a
menu in a fast-food restaurant. Ask each other about the prices.

A HOT DOG	$1.75
A HAMBURGER	$2.25
A CHEESEBURGER	
A TACO	$1.50
A SANDWICH	$4.35
LEMONADE	
COFFEE	$ .95
TEA	
MILK	

How much is a hot dog?

A hot dog is $1.75.

141

PUT IT TOGETHER · PART **B**

Work with a partner. You each have different information about a menu in a fast-food restaurant. Ask each other about the prices.

How much is a hot dog?

A hot dog is $1.75.

A HOT DOG	$1.75
A HAMBURGER	
A CHEESEBURGER	$2.60
A TACO	
A SANDWICH	
LEMONADE	$1.25
COFFEE	
TEA	$ .95
MILK	$1.15

VOCABULARY FOUNDATIONS

ATM card	air letter
bank	envelope
bank account	mailing address
bank book	money order
bills	package
change	post office
check	registered letter
checkbook	registered mail
coins	return address
credit card	stamps
deposit slip	window
withdrawal slip	

LANGUAGE SKILL FOUNDATIONS

I can . . .

☐ identify bank items
☐ identify banks in the community
☐ write checks
☐ identify postal items
☐ obtain post office services
☐ identify mailing address and return address on an envelope
☐ find out local post office hours
☐ make change
☐ tell ways to save money
☐ identify coins and bills from different countries
☐ identify prices on a fast-food menu

Talk About It! ▶▶▶ What are these people doing? What are they saying?

Unit 11

Health

Vocabulary Preview

1 head	4 nose	7 stomach	10 finger
2 eye	5 neck	8 arm	11 leg
3 ear	6 back	9 hand	12 foot

Goals

▶ **Parts of the body**

▶ **Ailments**

▶ **Medicine**

▶ **Making a doctor's appointment**

▶ **Staying healthy**

▶ **Dosage information on medicine labels**

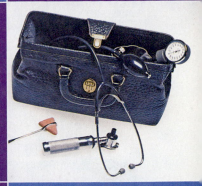

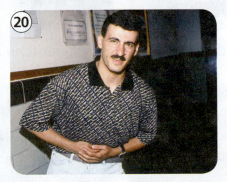

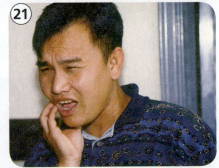

13 backache	**16** earache	**19** sore throat
14 cold	**17** fever	**20** stomachache
15 cough	**18** headache	**21** toothache

A. What's the matter?

B. I have a headache.

Practice conversations with a partner.

A. What's the matter?

B. I have _____.

1. a stomachache

2. a backache

3. an earache

4. a toothache

5. a sore throat

6. a cold

7. a cough

8. a fever

Grammar   Write the correct word.

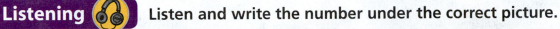

| I You } | **have** a headache. | He She } | **has** a headache. |

1. She ___has___ a stomachache.

2. I _____ a toothache.

3. He _____ a cold.

4. I _____ a sore throat.

5. You _____ a cough.

6. She _____ an earache.

Listening   Listen and write the number under the correct picture.

___   ___   ___   _1_   ___

Parts of the Body

Practice conversations with other students.

A. What's the matter?

B. My _____ hurts.

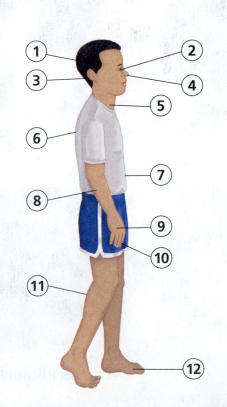

1 head		**7** stomach	
2 eye		**8** arm	
3 ear		**9** hand	
4 nose		**10** finger	
5 neck		**11** leg	
6 back		**12** foot	

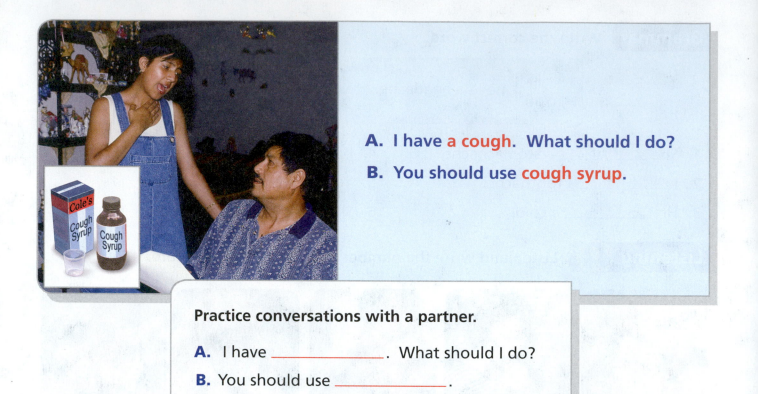

A. I have **a cough.** What should I do?

B. You should use **cough syrup.**

Practice conversations with a partner.

A. I have _____. What should I do?

B. You should use _____.

1. aspirin

2. ear drops

3. cold medicine

4. antacid tablets

5. throat lozenges

Listening

Listen and write the number next to the correct medicine.

 ___   1   ___  ___

Matching

1. When I have an earache, I use   cold medicine.

2. When I have a cough, I use   antacid tablets.

3. When I have a cold, I use   cough syrup.

4. When I have a stomachache, I use   throat lozenges.

5. When I have a sore throat, I use   ear drops.

Where can I find cough syrup?

A. Excuse me. Where can I find **cough syrup**?

B. Look in Aisle **1**.

A. Thank you.

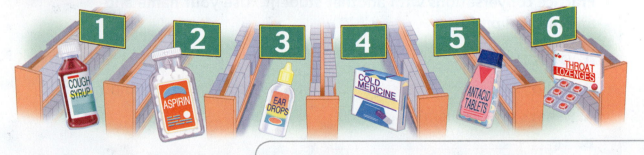

Look at the drug store diagram. Practice conversations with other students.

A. Excuse me. Where can I find _____?

B. Look in Aisle ___.

A. Thank you.

A. Doctor's Office.

B. Hello. This is **Alan Wong**. I want to make an appointment.

A. What's the problem?

B. **I have a bad stomachache**.

A. Can you come in tomorrow at **2:15**?

B. Yes. That's fine.

Practice conversations with another student. Use your name and any medical problem.

A. Doctor's Office.

B. Hello. This is _____. I want to make an appointment.

A. What's the problem?

B. _____.

A. Can you come in tomorrow at _____?

B. Yes. That's fine.

Listening  Listen and write the number under the correct picture.

____   ____   ____   ____   _1_

What happened? Practice conversations about these injuries.

> **A.** What happened?
>
> **B.** I _____.
>
> **A.** I'm sorry to hear that.

1. broke my arm

2. broke my leg

3. sprained my wrist

4. cut my finger

5. cut my face

6. burned my hand

Community Connections

Go to a local drug store. Ask questions.
Fill in the chart with names of medicines.

What do you recommend for _____?

I recommend Boyer Aspirin.

a headache	
a stomachache	
a sore throat	
a backache	
a cold	
a cough	
an earache	

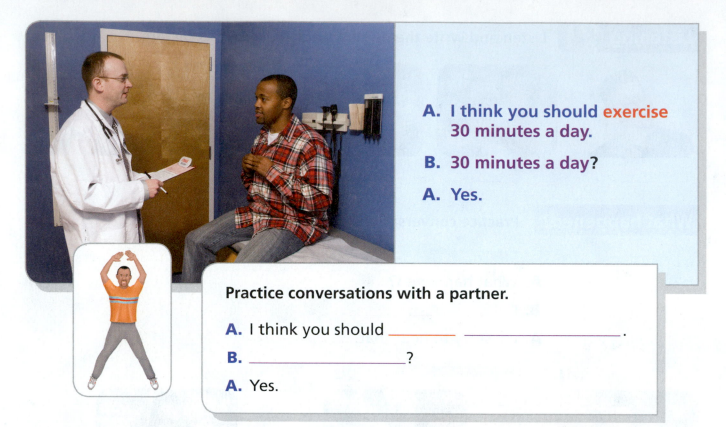

A. I think you should **exercise** 30 minutes a day.

B. 30 minutes a day?

A. Yes.

Practice conversations with a partner.

A. I think you should _____ _____.

B. _____?

A. Yes.

1. eat 3 healthy meals a day

2. drink 6 glasses of water a day

3. take 1 vitamin every day

4. sleep 8 hours every night

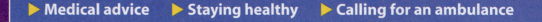

Cloze Reading   Write the missing words.

drink	eat	exercise	go	sleep	take

I try to stay healthy. I _____eat_____ ¹ three healthy meals a day.

I _____ ² five or six glasses of water a day. I _____ ³

a vitamin every morning. I _____ ⁴ thirty minutes a day. I _____ ⁵

seven hours every night, and I _____ ⁶ to the doctor every year for a checkup.

Language in *Motion*   Health Survey

Move around the classroom. Ask four students questions. Fill in the chart.

	Name:	Name:	Name:	Name:
How many meals a day do you eat?				
How many glasses of water do you drink each day?				
How many times a week do you exercise?				
How many minutes do you exercise?				
How many hours do you sleep at night?				
Do you take a vitamin every day?				
Do you go to the doctor every year for a checkup?				

Now talk with your classmates about the health survey.

Calling for an Ambulance   Practice conversations with other students.

A. Emergency Operator.

B. My _____ just fell and hurt his/her head very badly. He/She can't move. Please send an ambulance.

A. What's your address?

B. _____.

A. And your telephone number?

B. _____.

A. Okay. An ambulance is on the way.

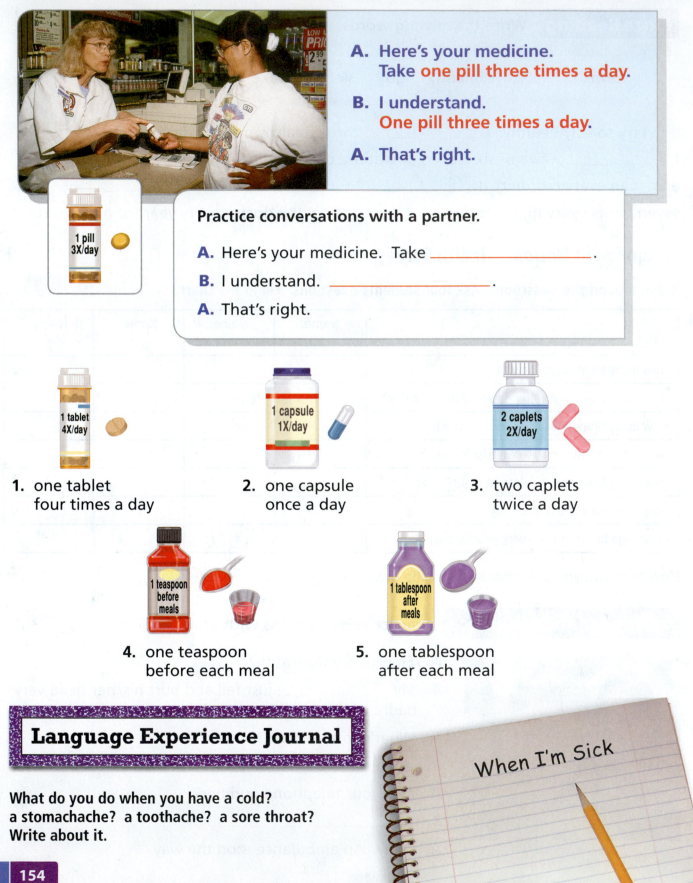

A. Here's your medicine.
Take **one pill three times a day.**

B. I understand.
One pill three times a day.

A. That's right.

1 pill
3X/day

Practice conversations with a partner.

A. Here's your medicine. Take _____.

B. I understand. _____.

A. That's right.

1 tablet
4X/day

1. one tablet
four times a day

1 capsule
1X/day

2. one capsule
once a day

2 caplets
2X/day

3. two caplets
twice a day

1 teaspoon
before
meals

4. one teaspoon
before each meal

1 tablespoon
after
meals

5. one tablespoon
after each meal

Language Experience Journal

What do you do when you have a cold?
a stomachache? a toothache? a sore throat?
Write about it.

When I'm Sick

Different Cultures / Different Ways

Different cultures have different remedies for common medical problems.

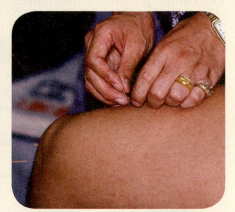

What remedies do you see? What medical problems are they for?
What are some remedies for medical problems in your culture?

PUT IT TOGETHER : PART A

INFORMATION GAP ACTIVITY

Work with a partner. You each have different information about a drug store. Ask each other questions to find the medicines.

Where can I find aspirin?

Look in Aisle 3.

ASPIRIN	3
COLD MEDICINE	4
EAR DROPS	
EYE DROPS	
COUGH SYRUP	4
ANTACID TABLETS	
THROAT LOZENGES	1

Work with a partner. You each have different information about a drug store. Ask each other questions to find the medicines.

ASPIRIN	3
COLD MEDICINE	
EAR DROPS	2
EYE DROPS	5
COUGH SYRUP	
ANTACID TABLETS	6
THROAT LOZENGES	

Where can I find aspirin?

Look in Aisle 3.

VOCABULARY FOUNDATIONS

arm	backache	antacid tablets
back	cold	aspirin
ear	cough	cold medicine
eye	earache	cough syrup
face	fever	ear drops
finger	headache	throat lozenges
foot	sore throat	vitamin
hand	stomachache	
head	toothache	caplet
leg		capsule
neck	broke	pill
nose	burned	tablet
stomach	cut	teaspoon
wrist	hurt	tablespoon
	sprained	

LANGUAGE SKILL FOUNDATIONS

I can . . .
- ☐ name common ailments
- ☐ identify parts of the body
- ☐ name common medicines
- ☐ locate medicines in a drug store
- ☐ make a doctor's appointment
- ☐ name common medical injuries
- ☐ ask a pharmacist for advice about medicines
- ☐ identify ways to stay healthy
- ☐ identify dosages on medicine labels
- ☐ compare remedies for medical problems in different cultures

Talk About It! ▶▶▶ What's the matter with these people? What are they saying?

School

Vocabulary Preview

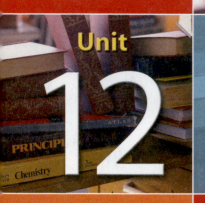

1 English teacher	5 school librarian	8 auditorium	12 office
2 P.E. teacher	6 school nurse	9 cafeteria	13 principal's office
3 principal	7 custodian	10 gym	14 nurse's office
4 guidance counselor		11 library	15 guidance office

16	English	**20**	art	**23**	band	**27**	basketball
17	math	**21**	music	**24**	choir	**28**	football
18	science	**22**	technology	**25**	drama	**29**	soccer
19	social studies			**26**	orchestra		

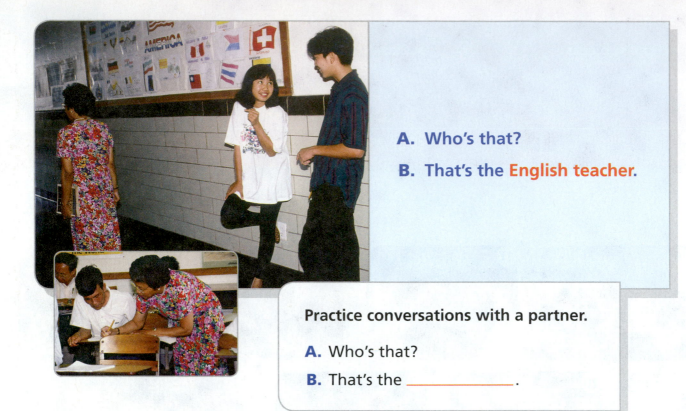

A. **Who's that?**

B. **That's the English teacher.**

Practice conversations with a partner.

A. Who's that?

B. That's the _____.

1. principal

2. school nurse

3. P.E. teacher

4. guidance counselor

5. custodian

6. school librarian

Places at School

Practice conversations with a partner.

A. Where are you going?

B. I'm going to the _____.

1. library

2. cafeteria

3. gym

4. auditorium

5. office

6. principal's office

7. nurse's office

8. guidance office

Which people in this lesson work in your school? What are their names? Where do they work?

Matching

1. The principal is in the   nurse's office.

2. The librarian is in the   gym.

3. The school nurse is in the   library.

4. The guidance counselor is in the   principal's office.

5. The P.E. teacher is in the   guidance office.

A. What's your favorite subject?

B. Math.

Practice conversations with a partner.

A. What's your favorite subject?

B. _____.

1. English

2. social studies

3. science

4. art

5. music

6. technology

Listening  Listen and write the number under the correct picture.

_____

_____

__1__

_____

_____

_____

Unscramble the Subjects

1. rta   ___art___
2. htam   _____
3. miscu   _____

4. secnice   _____
5. gishlEn   _____
6. logonchety _____

Language in *Motion*

Move around the classroom. Ask eight students. Fill in the chart.

What's your favorite subject?

	Name	Favorite Subject
1.		
2.		
3.		
4.		
5.		
6.		
7.		
8.		

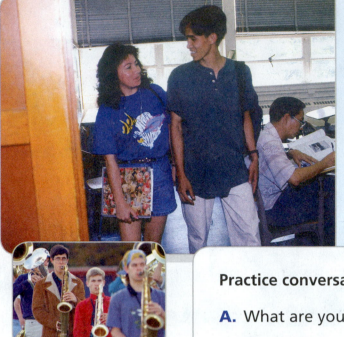

A. What are you going to do after school today?

B. I have band **practice.**

Practice conversations with a partner.

A. What are you going to do after school today?

B. I have _____ practice.

1. orchestra

2. choir

3. drama

4. football

5. soccer

6. basketball

Listening  Listen and write the number under the correct picture.

_____

_____

_____

1

_____

_____

School Vocabulary Circle the correct word.

1. The band practices (art (music)) every day after school.

2. My daughter has drama practice in the (guidance office   auditorium) today.

3. The (counselor   custodian) is cleaning the tables in the cafeteria.

4. I have a bad stomachache. I'm going to the (nurse's   principal's) office.

5. My son has (basketball   football) practice in the gym after school today.

6. The students exercise twice a week in their (P.E.   science) class.

Community Connections

What different types of schools are there in your community? What are the names of the schools? Where are they? Who goes to these schools? Discuss with other students.

Name of School	Location	Students

A. What class do you have **first** period?

B. **English**.

A. In which classroom?

B. Room **two fifteen**.

Practice conversations about this class schedule.

A. What class do you have _____ period?

B. _____ .

A. In which classroom?

B. Room _____ .

Period	Class	Teacher	Room
1st	English	Ms. Wilson	215
2nd	Science	Mrs. Ramos	124
3rd	Math	Mr. Adler	319
4th	Social Studies	Miss Chen	222
5th	Technology	Mr. Davis	18
6th	Music	Ms. Caruso	132

Language Experience Journal

Write about your school. Describe it.
Tell about the places and the people.

My School

Different Cultures / Different Ways

Schools in different countries around the world can be very different.

Tell about schools in your country.
Describe the school buildings and classrooms.
Describe the subjects and the activities.
What are the differences between schools in different countries?

PUT IT TOGETHER : PART A

Work with a partner. You each have different information about this school schedule.
Ask each other questions to complete the schedule.

INFORMATION GAP ACTIVITY

What time is science class?

From 8:15 to 9:00.

science	8:15–9:00
math	9:05–9:50
social studies	
English	10:45–11:30
technology	
music	
art	1:40–2:25

PUT IT TOGETHER : PART B

Work with a partner. You each have different information about this school schedule.
Ask each other questions to complete the schedule.

science	8:15–9:00
math	
social studies	9:55–10:40
English	
technology	12:00–12:45
music	12:50–1:35
art	

What time is science class?

From 8:15 to 9:00.

VOCABULARY FOUNDATIONS

custodian	art
English teacher	English
guidance counselor	math
P.E. teacher	music
principal	science
school librarian	social studies
school nurse	technology
auditorium	band
cafeteria	basketball
guidance office	choir
gym	drama
library	football
nurse's office	orchestra
office	soccer
principal's office	

LANGUAGE SKILL FOUNDATIONS

I can . . .

- ☐ name school personnel
- ☐ name places in a school
- ☐ name school subjects
- ☐ name extracurricular activities
- ☐ describe different types of schools in my community
- ☐ read a class schedule
- ☐ describe the places and people in my school
- ☐ compare schools in different countries

am
is
are

COLLEGE

STATE COLLEGE

Talk About It! ▶ ▶ ▶ **What places and people do you see? What are the people doing?**

Vocabulary Preview

1 assembler

2 baker

3 barber

4 bus driver

5 carpenter

6 cashier

7 construction worker

8 cook

9 custodian

10 delivery person

11 doctor

12 electrician

13 gardener

14 housekeeper

Goals

▶ **Occupations**

▶ **Job skills**

▶ **Help Wanted signs & want ads**

▶ **Places at work**

▶ **Safety warnings & signs**

▶ **Work schedules & paychecks**

15 mechanic	**19** police officer	**23** security guard	**27** waiter
16 painter	**20** repairperson	**24** taxi driver	**28** waitress
17 pharmacist	**21** salesperson	**25** teacher	
18 plumber	**22** secretary	**26** truck driver	

A. What do you do?

B. I'm a cook.

Practice conversations with a partner.

A. What do you do?

B. I'm _____.

1. a custodian

2. a gardener

3. a cashier

4. an electrician

5. a repairperson

6. a delivery person

7. a security guard

8. a police officer

9. a construction worker

What kind of job are you looking for?

Practice conversations about the jobs on page 172.

A. What kind of job are you looking for?

B. I'm looking for a job as _____.

Listening

Listen and write the number under the correct Help Wanted sign.

BOB'S DINER
Cook Wanted

_____

Cashiers Wanted

1

Help Wanted

_____

Delivery Help Wanted

_____

Custodian Needed

_____

Gardener Wanted

_____

Missing Letters

1. c _a_ sh _i_ er
2. cu __ __ o __ ian
3. e __ ect __ icia __
4. __ ar __ ente __
5. r __ pai __ per __ on
6. p __ li __ e o __ __ ice __
7. s __ c __ ri __ y gua __ __
8. de __ i __ er __ p __ r __ o __

A. Can you **drive a bus?**

B. Yes, I can. I'm an experienced **bus driver.**

Practice conversations with a partner.

A. Can you _____?

B. Yes, I can. I'm an experienced _____.

1. paint
painter

2. teach
teacher

3. bake
baker

4. type
secretary

5. drive a taxi
taxi driver

6. drive a truck
truck driver

7. fix sinks
plumber

8. fix cars
mechanic

9. repair buildings
carpenter

What can you do?

Practice conversations about the job skills on page 174.

A. Tell me about your job skills.
What can you do?

B. I can _____ .

Listening

Listen and write the number under the correct want ad.

SECRETARY	BAKER	PAINTER	MECHANIC	TAXI DRIVER
_____	_____	_____	_____	**1**

Matching

1. I'm a bus driver.
2. I'm a painter.
3. I'm a plumber.
4. I'm a secretary.
5. I'm a mechanic.
6. I'm a carpenter.

I can paint.
I can fix cars.
I can repair buildings.
I can type.
I can drive a bus.
I can fix sinks.

Language in *Motion*

Pantomime a job skill.
Ask other students:
"What can I do?"
"What's my job?"

You can type!

You're a secretary!

You can drive a truck!

You're a truck driver!

A. **What's your occupation?**

B. **I'm a waitress.**

A. **Where do you work?**

B. **At Betty's Restaurant.**

Practice conversations with a partner.

A. What's your occupation?

B. I'm _____ .

A. Where do you work?

B. At _____ .

1. a waiter
Danny's Restaurant

2. a housekeeper
the Midtown Hotel

3. an assembler
Apex Electronics

4. a doctor
Memorial Hospital

5. a salesperson
J-Mart Department
Store

6. a pharmacist
Save-Rite Pharmacy

Reading: Want Ads

HELP WANTED

TRUCK DRIVER
Express Package Company.
1200 Central Ave.
Call 684-2222.

COOK
New restaurant in city center.
Call Dan at 974-3500.

SECRETARY
Lopez Insurance.
570 Main St. 663-2777.

CUSTODIAN
A-1 Building Services.
Full-time & part-time.
668-4950.

MECHANIC
Sal's Service Station.
4375 Central Ave.
684-9733.

What numbers should they call?

1. Ricky can clean offices.
   _____

2. Marta can cook very well.
   _____

3. Alfonso can drive a truck.
   _____

4. Brenda can fix cars.
   _____

5. Stella can type.
   _____

Job Application Form Fill out the form with your information.

APPLICATION FOR EMPLOYMENT

Name: _____ Social Security No.: _____

Street: _____ Apartment: _____

City: _____ State: _____ Zip Code: _____ Telephone: _____

Work Experience (Start with present or most recent employer):

Job	Company	From	To

Date: _____ Signature: _____

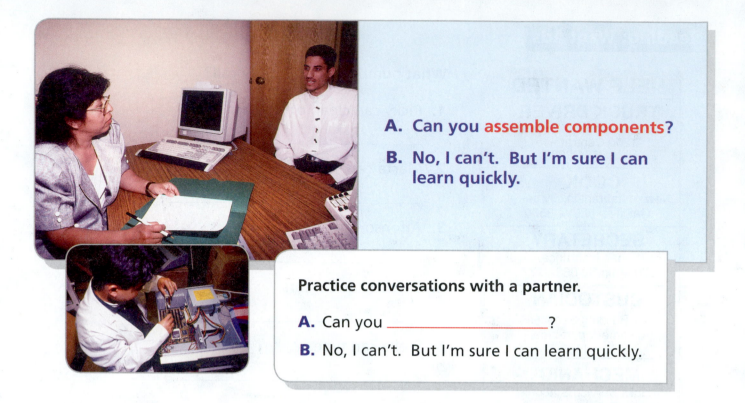

A. Can you **assemble components**?

B. No, I can't. But I'm sure I can learn quickly.

Practice conversations with a partner.

A. Can you _____?

B. No, I can't. But I'm sure I can learn quickly.

1. cook

2. sell clothing

3. cut hair

4. repair watches

5. operate equipment

6. use a cash register

I can't come to work today.

Practice conversations with a partner.

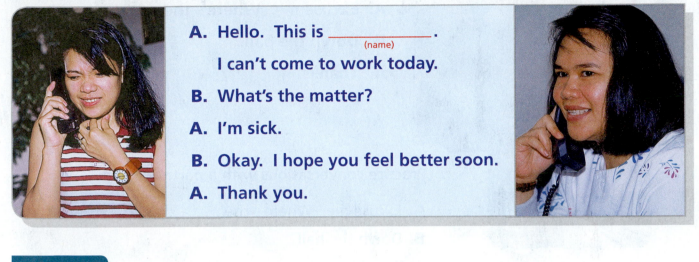

A. Hello. This is _____.
(name)

I can't come to work today.

B. What's the matter?

A. I'm sick.

B. Okay. I hope you feel better soon.

A. Thank you.

Grammar

> can   can't

1. Yes. I _____*can*_____ cook.

2. No. I _____ repair watches.

3. I'm sure I _____ learn quickly.

4. _____ you use a cash register?

5. Yes, I _____.

6. I'm sick. I _____ come to work today.

Language in *Motion*

Move around the classroom. Ask students questions. Write their names.

Can you _____?

No, I can't.

Yes, I can.

assemble things	
repair things	
use a cash register	
operate equipment	
cook	
type	
drive a truck	

A. Excuse me. Where's the **supply room**?

B. Down the hall.

A. Thanks.

Practice conversations with a partner.

A. Excuse me. Where's the _____?

B. Down the hall.

A. Thanks.

1. cafeteria

2. mailroom

3. bathroom

4. employee lounge

5. personnel office

6. vending machine

A Workplace Diagram   Look at the diagram and answer the questions.

1. It's across from the supply room. _____cafeteria_____

2. It's across from the personnel office. _____

3. It's next to the personnel office. _____

4. It's between the mailroom and the bathroom. _____

5. It's across from the mailroom. _____

Community ▶ Connections

Look for two Help Wanted signs in your community. Write down what you see, and write the names of the workplaces. Discuss these jobs and workplaces with other students.

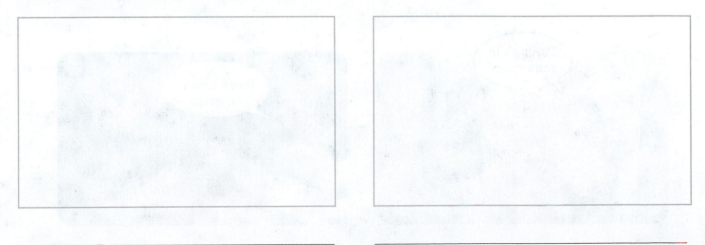

Workplace _____   Workplace _____

The floor is wet!

A. Careful!

B. Excuse me?

A. The floor is wet!

B. Okay. Thanks for telling me.

Practice conversations with a partner.

A. Careful!

B. Excuse me?

A. _____

B. Okay. Thanks for telling me.

Put on your safety glasses!

1.

Don't stand there!

2.

Don't go in that room!

3.

Don't smoke in here!

4.

Safety Signs at Work **Match the signs and sentences.**

1. Wear safety glasses.

2. The floor is wet.

3. Don't smoke.

4. Wear a helmet.

5. Don't go that way.

6. Don't stand there.

What other safety signs do you see in school, at work, or in the community?
Draw three signs and write their meanings. Then discuss with other students.

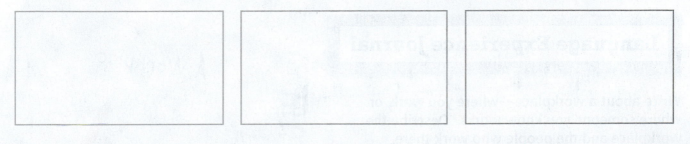

Day	SUN	MON	TUE	WED	THU	FRI	SAT
Start	12:00 PM	9:00 AM	9:00 AM		5:00 PM	9:00 AM	10:00 AM
End	5:00 PM	5:00 PM	5:00 PM		9:00 PM	5:00 PM	5:00 PM

This is Yolanda's work schedule. She works __6__ [1] days a week. She doesn't work on _____. [2] On Saturday she works ____ [3] hours. On Sunday she works ____ [4] hours. On Monday, Tuesday, and Friday she works ____ [5] hours a day. She works in the evening on _____. [6] She works a total of ____ [7] hours a week.

Wilson's Department Store		Mercado, Y.		EMP. NO. 00427	
PAY PERIOD ENDING	RATE	HOURS		GROSS PAY	
10 05 09	13.00/hour	40		$520.00	
FED TAX 52.00				GROSS PAY	$520.00
FICA/MED 41.60				DEDUCTIONS	$144.10
STATE TAX 26.00					
HEALTH 24.50				NET PAY	$375.90

WILSON'S DEPARTMENT STORE   Check No.   4377291

Pay to **YOLANDA MERCADO**   Date Issued   10 08 09

THREE HUNDRED SEVENTY-FIVE DOLLARS AND NINETY CENTS ———— $375.90

Marjorie Denton

This is Yolanda's paycheck. She makes _____ [8] an hour. Her gross pay for the week is _____ [9], but Yolanda doesn't take home this amount because there are deductions from her paycheck. She pays _____ [10] for federal taxes, _____ [11] for social security (FICA) and Medicare taxes, _____ [12] for state taxes, and _____ [13] for her company's health plan. After these deductions, Yolanda takes home _____ [14].

Language Experience Journal

A Workplace

Write about a workplace—where you work, or where someone you know works. Describe the workplace and the people who work there.

Different Cultures   Different Ways

Men and women sometimes have different jobs in different cultures.

In your culture, what jobs do women usually have? What jobs do men usually have? Is this changing?

As a class, compare men's and women's jobs in different cultures.

PUT IT TOGETHER PART A

INFORMATION GAP ACTIVITY

Work with a partner. First, check (✓) the job skills you have. Then ask each other about your skills.

You		Your Partner
_____	cook	_____
_____	type	_____
_____	fix cars	_____
_____	drive a truck	_____
_____	repair furniture	_____
_____	operate equipment	_____
_____	use a cash register	_____

Can you cook?

Yes. I can.
No, I can't.

PUT IT TOGETHER : PART B

Work with a partner. First, check (✓) the job skills you have. Then ask each other about your skills.

"Can you cook?"

"Yes. I can. No, I can't."

You		Your Partner
_____	cook	_____
_____	type	_____
_____	fix cars	_____
_____	drive a truck	_____
_____	repair furniture	_____
_____	operate equipment	_____
_____	use a cash register	_____

VOCABULARY FOUNDATIONS

assembler	police officer	teach
baker	repairperson	type
barber	salesperson	use
bus driver	secretary	
carpenter	security	bathroom
cashier	guard	cafeteria
construction	taxi driver	employee
worker	teacher	lounge
cook	truck driver	helmet
custodian	waiter	mailroom
delivery	waitress	paycheck
person		personnel
doctor	bake	office
electrician	cook	safety
gardener	cut	glasses
housekeeper	drive	supply
mechanic	fix	room
painter	operate	vending
pharmacist	paint	machine
plumber	repair	work
	sell	schedule

LANGUAGE SKILL FOUNDATIONS

I can . . .
- ☐ name occupations
- ☐ interpret Help Wanted signs
- ☐ describe job skills
- ☐ name places of employment
- ☐ interpret want ads
- ☐ fill out a job application form
- ☐ call in sick
- ☐ locate places and facilities at work
- ☐ interpret a workplace diagram
- ☐ give and understand safety warnings
- ☐ interpret warning & safety signs
- ☐ interpret a work schedule
- ☐ intepret a paycheck & pay stub
- ☐ compare men's and women's jobs in different cultures

Today's Specials

BUS STOP

555•LAWN

PIZZA

Vocabulary Preview

1 walk

2 drive a car

3 ride a bicycle

4 take a bus

5 take a subway

6 take a taxi

7 bus schedule

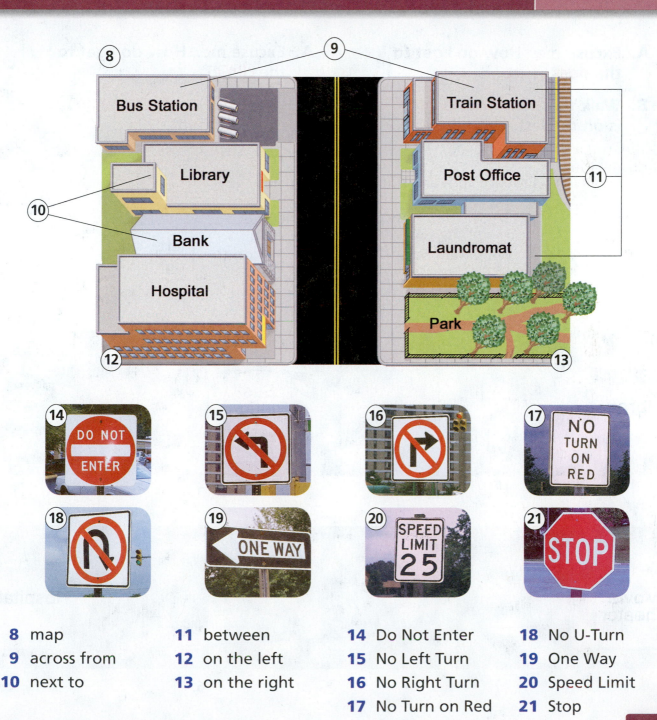

8 map	**11** between	**14** Do Not Enter	**18** No U-Turn
9 across from	**12** on the left	**15** No Left Turn	**19** One Way
10 next to	**13** on the right	**16** No Right Turn	**20** Speed Limit
		17 No Turn on Red	**21** Stop

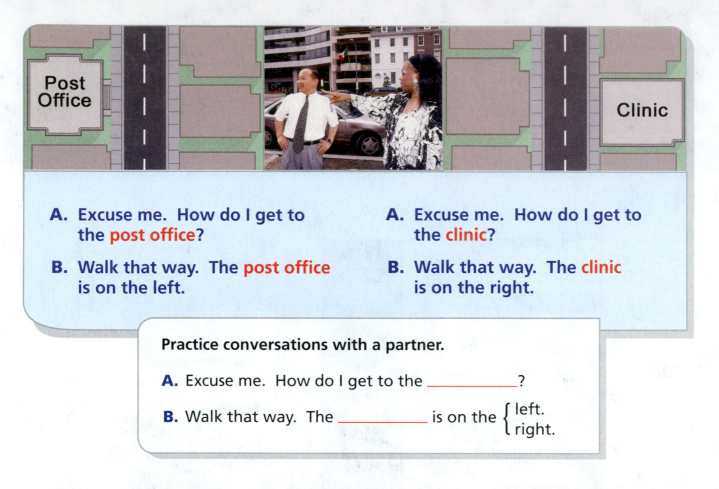

Post Office

Clinic

A. Excuse me. How do I get to the **post office**?

B. Walk that way. The **post office** is on the left.

A. Excuse me. How do I get to the **clinic**?

B. Walk that way. The **clinic** is on the right.

Practice conversations with a partner.

A. Excuse me. How do I get to the _____?

B. Walk that way. The _____ is on the $\begin{cases} \text{left.} \\ \text{right.} \end{cases}$

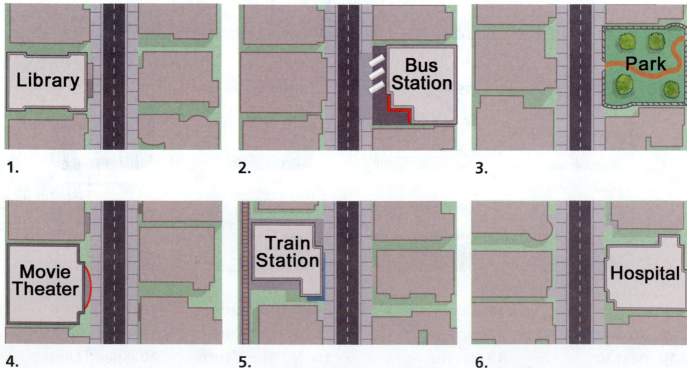

Library

1.

Bus Station

2.

Park

3.

Movie Theater

4.

Train Station

5.

Hospital

6.

Where Is It?   **Look at the map and answer the questions.**

across from	between	left	next to	right

1. The bus station is on the _____ *left* _____ .

2. The park is on the _____ .

3. The library is _____ the post office.

4. The bank is _____ the hospital.

5. The laundromat is _____ the post office and the park.

Listening 🎧

Look at the map above. Listen and circle the correct place.

1. (library)	post office	**5.** park	laundromat
2. hospital	laundromat	**6.** library	bus station
3. bank	park	**7.** hospital	laundromat
4. library	train station	**8.** bank	bus station

A. Excuse me. How do I get to the **mall**?

B. Take Bus Number **7**.

A. Bus Number **7**? Thank you.

Practice conversations with a partner.

A. Excuse me. How do I get to the _____?

B. Take Bus Number ____.

A. Bus Number ____? Thank you.

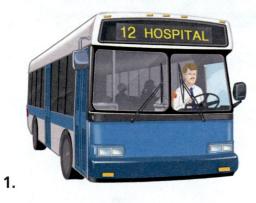

1.

2.

3.

4.

Take the Blue Line.

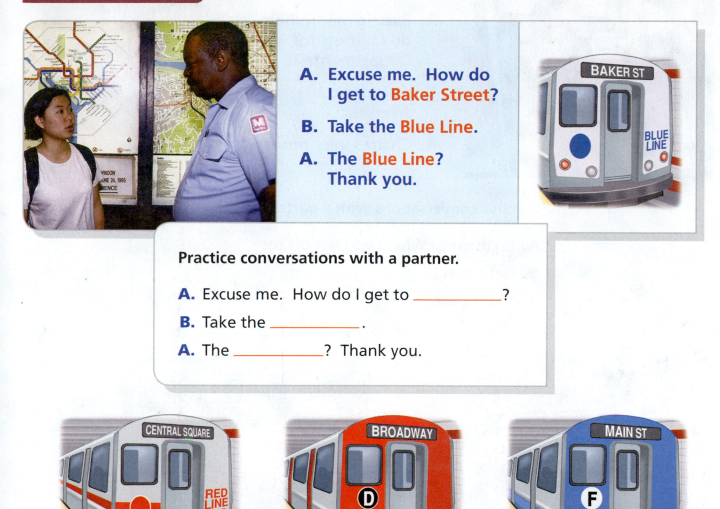

A. Excuse me. How do I get to **Baker Street**?

B. Take the **Blue Line**.

A. The **Blue Line**? Thank you.

Practice conversations with a partner.

A. Excuse me. How do I get to _____?

B. Take the _____.

A. The _____? Thank you.

1.   2.   3.

Now practice more conversations about public transportation in your community.

Listening

Listen and write the number under the correct picture.

_____   1   _____   _____

A. Excuse me. Where do I get off for **Mal's Department Store**?

B. Get off at **Jackson Avenue**.

A. Thanks very much.

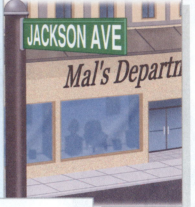

Practice conversations with a partner.

A. Excuse me. Where do I get off for _____?

B. Get off at _____.

A. Thanks very much.

1. the Midtown Clinic

2. Central Park

3. the East Town Mall

4. the main post office

Now practice more conversations about places in your community.

Listening   Listen and write the number under the correct sign.

_____   _____   <u>1</u>   _____   _____

Language in *Motion* Survey

Do a class survey. Ask all the students. Count the answers.

	Number of Students
walk	
take a bus	
take a subway	
take a taxi	
drive a car	
ride a bicycle	

Community Connections

Where do you go on public transportation? How do you get there? What's the route number? Where do you get off? Give information about four places.

Place	Transportation	Route Number	Location
City Hall	bus	M12	Center Street

A. **Slow down!**

B. **What?**

A. **Slow down!**
The sign says,
"Speed Limit 30."

B. **Thanks.**

Practice conversations with a partner.

A. _____

B. What?

A. _____
The sign says, "_____."

B. Thanks.

1. Slow down!

2. You have to stop!

3. You can't go that way!

4. You're driving too fast!

5. You can't go on that street!

6. Don't turn yet!

Traffic Signs   Match the signs and sentences.

1.   No right turn.

2.   No U-turn.

3.   No left turn.

4.   Look for people in the street.

5.   There's a school nearby.

6.   There are train tracks ahead.

What other traffic signs do you see in your community? Draw three signs and write their meanings. Then discuss with other students.

Route 2B				
Center Street	River Road	Lee Avenue	School Street	Wilson Avenue
Weekdays				
6:00 AM	6:15	6:30	6:40	6:50
6:30	6:45	7:00	7:10	7:20
7:00	7:15	7:30	7:40	7:50
7:30	7:45	8:00	8:10	8:20
8:00	8:15	8:30	8:40	8:50
9:00	9:15	9:30	9:40	9:50
10:00	10:15	10:30	10:40	10:50
12:00 PM	12:15	12:30	12:40	12:50
2:00	2:15	2:30	2:40	2:50
4:00	4:15	4:30	4:40	4:50
5:00	5:15	5:30	5:40	5:50
5:30	5:45	6:00	6:10	6:20
6:00	6:15	6:30	6:40	6:50
6:30	6:45	7:00	7:10	7:20
7:00	7:15	7:30	7:40	7:50
8:00	8:15	8:30	8:40	8:50

This is the bus schedule for Bus Number 2B. It goes from Center Street to Wilson Avenue.

The **first** bus in the morning **leaves** Center Street at 6:00. It **arrives** at River Road at 6:15.

The **next** bus leaves Center Street at 6:30. It arrives at Lee Avenue at 7:00.

The **last** bus leaves Center Street at 8:00. It arrives at School Street at 8:40.

1. The first bus arrives at Wilson Avenue at ___6:50___.

2. The next bus arrives at Wilson Avenue at _____.

3. The last bus arrives at Lee Avenue at _____.

4. The last bus arrives at School Street at _____.

5. It's 1:30 PM. The next bus leaves Center Street at _____.

6. It's 6:00 PM. The next bus arrives at River Road at _____.

7. The last bus leaves Center Street at _____.

8. The last bus arrives at Wilson Avenue at _____.

Language Experience Journal

How do you get to places? Do you walk? Do you drive? Do you take the bus or subway? Write about it.

Getting Places

Different Cultures / Different Ways

There are many types of transportation in different places around the world.

Tell about transportation in your country.
How do people get places?

PUT IT TOGETHER : PART A

INFORMATION GAP ACTIVITY

Work with a partner. You each have different information about the same inter-city bus schedule. Ask each other questions to complete the schedule.

DEPARTURES	
SAN DIEGO	9:30
SAN FRANCISCO	10:15
LAS VEGAS	10:00
SACRAMENTO	
PORTLAND	11:15
DALLAS	
SALT LAKE CITY	12:00

When does the bus to San Diego leave?

It leaves at 9:30.

INFORMATION GAP ACTIVITY

Work with a partner. You each have different information about the same inter-city bus schedule. Ask each other questions to complete the schedule.

When does the bus to San Diego leave?

It leaves at 9:30.

DEPARTURES

SAN DIEGO	9:30
SAN FRANCISCO	
LAS VEGAS	
SACRAMENTO	9:45
PORTLAND	
DALLAS	11:30
SALT LAKE CITY	

VOCABULARY FOUNDATIONS

across from	bicycle
between	bus
next to	bus schedule
on the left	car
on the right	map
	sign
arrive	subway
drive a car	taxi
get off	traffic sign
get to	
leave	Do Not Enter
ride	No Left Turn
take a *bus*	No Right Turn
take Bus Number *7*	No Turn on Red
take the *Blue* Line	No U-Turn
take the *D* Train	One Way
walk	Speed Limit
	Stop

LANGUAGE SKILL FOUNDATIONS

I can . . .
- ☐ locate places
- ☐ ask for & give directions
- ☐ interpret a simple map of a street
- ☐ identify types of public transportation
- ☐ ask for & give information
- ☐ ask about a destination on public transportation
- ☐ identify traffic signs
- ☐ give driving safety warnings
- ☐ interpret a bus schedule
- ☐ describe how to get to places in the community
- ☐ compare transportation in different countries

Recreation & Entertainment

Vocabulary Preview

1 exercise
2 go dancing
3 go jogging

4 go rollerblading
5 go swimming
6 go to a ballgame

7 go to a concert
8 go to a museum
9 go to the park
10 go to the zoo

▶ **Recreation & entertainment activities**

▶ **Expressing likes**

▶ **Expressing future plans**

▶ **Telling about past activities**

▶ **Calendars & schedules**

11 listen to music

12 play baseball

13 play basketball

14 play golf

15 play soccer

16 play tennis

17 see a movie

18 see a play

19 watch TV

A. What do you like to do in your free time?

B. I like to play soccer.

Practice conversations with a partner.

A. What do you like to do in your free time?

B. I like to _____.

1. play basketball

2. play tennis

3. watch TV

4. listen to music

5. exercise

6. go jogging

7. go swimming

8. go rollerblading

9. go dancing

Listening  Listen and write the number under the correct picture.

_1_ _____ _____ _____ _____

Matching

1. listen to   TV
2. watch   soccer
3. go   music
4. play   swimming

Missing Letters

1. s _o_ c c _e_ r
2. t ___ n n ___ s
3. ___ a s ___ e t ___ a l l
4. ___ x ___ r c ___ s e
5. s w ___ ___ m i ___ ___

Language in *Motion* Survey

Do a class survey. Ask all the students. Write and count the answers.

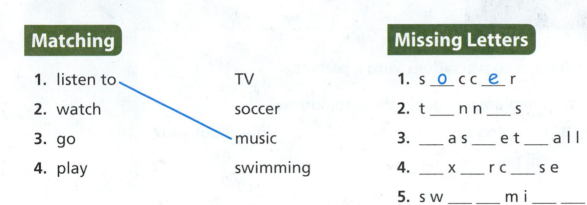

What do you like to do in your free time?

I like to _____.

Activity	Number of Students

A. What are you going to do tomorrow?

B. I'm going to see a movie. How about you?

A. I'm going to go to the park.

Practice conversations with a partner.

A. What are you going to do tomorrow?

B. I'm going to _____. How about you?

A. I'm going to _____.

1. see a play   go to a concert   **2.** play baseball   play golf

3. go jogging   go to a ballgame   **4.** go to a museum   go to the zoo

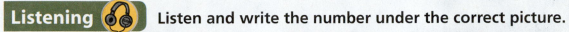

Listening

Listen and write the number under the correct picture.

_____   _____   _____   _____   1

Grammar

| are   do   go   going   I'm   to   you |

1. What are ___you___ going to do tomorrow?

   _____ going to see a movie.

2. What are you going to _____ tomorrow?

   I'm going _____ play baseball.

3. What _____ you going to do tomorrow?

   I'm _____ to _____ to a concert.

Community Connections

Where can you do these activities in your community? Fill in the names of the places.

Activity	Place	Activity	Place
play soccer		see a play	
play basketball		go to a concert	
see a movie		go dancing	
go swimming		go jogging	

A. What did you do yesterday?

B. I **went to a concert.**

Practice conversations with a partner.

A. What did you do yesterday?

B. I _____.

1. played soccer

2. watched TV

3. went to the park

4. listened to music

5. went to the zoo

6. saw a play

7. went dancing

8. played basketball

9. went jogging

Grammar

I like to **play** baseball.

I **played** baseball yesterday.

I like to **watch** TV.

I **watched** TV yesterday.

I like to **go** jogging.

I **went** jogging yesterday.

I like to **see** movies.

I **saw** a movie yesterday.

Circle the correct word.

1. I like to ((play) played) soccer.

2. I (play   played) soccer yesterday.

3. I (listen   listened) to music yesterday.

4. I like to (listen   listened) to music in the evening.

5. I (go   went) to the zoo yesterday.

6. I like to (go   went) to the park.

7. I (play   played) tennis yesterday.

8. I like to (exercise   exercised) in the morning.

9. I (exercise   exercised) yesterday morning.

10. I like to (go   went) dancing on Saturday night.

11. I (go   went) dancing yesterday.

12. I (see   saw) a play last weekend.

Listening   **Listen and circle the correct word.**

1.	go	went	5. go	went
2.	listen	listened	6. play	played
3.	exercise	exercised	7. go	went
4.	exercise	exercised	8. see	saw

JANUARY

SUN	MON	TUE	WED	THU	FRI	SAT
		1 WORK SWIMMING	2 WORK	3 WORK SWIMMING	4 WORK	5 DANCING
6 SOCCER	7 WORK	8 WORK SWIMMING	9 WORK	10 WORK SWIMMING	11 WORK CONCERT: CARTER HALL	12
13 SOCCER	14 WORK	15 WORK SWIMMING	16 WORK	17 WORK SWIMMING	18 WORK	19 DANCING
20 SOCCER	21 WORK	22 WORK SWIMMING	23 WORK	24 WORK SWIMMING	25 WORK PLAY: ESSEX THEATER	26 PLAY BASEBALL
27 SOCCER	28 WORK	29 WORK SWIMMING	30 WORK	31 WORK SWIMMING		

Circle the correct words to complete the story.

This is Martin's calendar for the month of January. Martin works (four (five))[1] days a week. Martin plays soccer (once   twice)[2] a week. He goes swimming (once   twice)[3] a week. On January (11th   25th)[4] he's going to go to a concert. On the (third   fourth)[5] Friday in January he's going to see a play. Martin plays baseball once a (week   month)[6]. He's going to go (swimming   dancing)[7] twice in January. He's going to play soccer (four   five)[8] times in January.

Make a calendar for this month. Write all your activities on the calendar.

Language Experience Journal

Next Weekend

What are you going to do next weekend? Write about it.

Different Cultures | Different Ways

People in different cultures spend their free time in different ways.

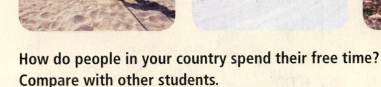

How do people in your country spend their free time?
Compare with other students.

PUT IT TOGETHER • PART A

INFORMATION GAP ACTIVITY

Work with a partner. You each have different information about Linda's schedule for tomorrow. Ask each other questions and fill in the calendar.

Daily Calendar   Saturday
                        2
                        May

8:00 AM	—	exercise
9:00	—	clean the apartment
10:00	—	_____
1:00 PM	—	have lunch with Amy
3:00	—	do the laundry
4:30	—	_____
6:00	—	cook dinner
7:30	—	_____

What's Linda going to do tomorrow at 8:00?

She's going to exercise.

Work with a partner. You each have different information about Linda's schedule for tomorrow. Ask each other questions and fill in the calendar.

Daily Calendar   Saturday 2 May

8:00 AM	—	exercise
9:00	—	_____
10:00	—	play tennis
1:00 PM	—	_____
3:00	—	_____
4:30	—	go jogging
6:00	—	_____
7:30	—	go dancing

VOCABULARY FOUNDATIONS

exercise	play baseball
go dancing	play basketball
go jogging	play golf
go rollerblading	play soccer
go swimming	play tennis
go to a ballgame	see a movie
go to a concert	see a play
go to a museum	watch TV
go to the park	
go to the zoo	free time
listen to music	tomorrow
	yesterday

LANGUAGE SKILL FOUNDATIONS

I can . . .

☐ name recreation & entertainment activities

☐ express what I like to do

☐ ask about people's free time activities

☐ ask about & express future plans

☐ identify places for recreation & entertainment in the community

☐ ask about & tell about past activities

☐ use a calendar

☐ write about future plans

☐ compare how people spend their free time in different cultures

☐ interpret a daily schedule

PAGE 6

Listen and circle.

1. A. What's your last name?
   B. Phan.
   A. How do you spell it?
   B. P-H-A-N.
2. A. What's your last name?
   B. Black.
   A. How do you spell it?
   B. B-L-A-C-K.
3. A. What's your last name?
   B. Clayton.
   A. How do you spell it?
   B. C-L-A-Y-T-O-N.
4. A. What's your last name?
   B. Green.
   A. How do you spell it?
   B. G-R-E-E-N.
5. A. What's your last name?
   B. Kramer.
   A. How do you spell it?
   B. K-R-A-M-E-R.
6. A. What's your last name?
   B. Sanchez.
   A. How do you spell it?
   B. S-A-N-C-H-E-Z.

PAGE 9

Listen and circle.

1. A. What's your telephone number?
   B. 249–1115.
   A. Is that 249–1115?
   B. Yes. That's correct.
2. A. What's your telephone number?
   B. 463–9221.
   A. Is that 463–9221?
   B. Yes. That's correct.
3. A. What's your telephone number?
   B. 948–6137.
   A. Is that 948–6137?
   B. Yes. That's correct.
4. A. What's your telephone number?
   B. 671–2098.
   A. Is that 671–2098?
   B. Yes. That's correct.
5. A. What's your telephone number?
   B. 728–0303.
   A. Is that 728–0303?
   B. Yes. That's correct.
6. A. What's your telephone number?
   B. 837–1284.
   A. Is that 837–1284?
   B. Yes. That's correct.

PAGE 11

Circle the apartment number you hear.

1. A. What's your apartment number?
   B. 6D.
   A. 6D?
   B. Yes. That's right.
2. A. What's your apartment number?
   B. 9J.
   A. 9J?
   B. Yes. That's right.
3. A. What's your apartment number?
   B. 1E.
   A. Did you say 1E?
   B. Yes. That's right.
4. A. What's your apartment number?
   B. 10K.
   A. Did you say 10K?
   B. Yes. That's correct.
5. A. What's your apartment number?
   B. 2D.
   A. 2D?
   B. Yes.
6. A. What's your apartment number?
   B. 8C.
   A. 8C?
   B. Yes. That's right.
7. A. What's your apartment number?
   B. 3E.
   A. Did you say 3E?
   B. Yes. That's right.

PAGE 23

Listen and write the number under the correct picture.

1. A. Is this your pencil?
   B. Yes. Thank you.
2. A. Is this your book?
   B. Yes. Thank you.
3. A. Is this your pen?
   B. Yes. Thank you.
4. A. Where's the bookshelf?
   B. Over there.
5. A. Is this your notebook?
   B. Yes. Thank you.

PAGE 27

Listen and write the number under the correct picture.

1. Go to the board.
2. Write your name.
3. Take out your book.
4. Raise your hand.
5. Open your book.
6. Erase your name.

PAGE 35

Listen and write the number under the correct picture.

1. Every day I brush my teeth.
2. Every day I read.
3. Every day I cook dinner.
4. Every day I go to work.
5. Every day I go to bed.

PAGE 37

Listen and write the number under the correct picture.

1. A. What are you doing?
   B. I'm ironing.
2. A. What are you doing?
   B. I'm exercising.
3. A. What are you doing?
   B. I'm watching TV.
4. A. What are you doing?
   B. I'm washing the dishes.
5. A. What are you doing?
   B. I'm feeding the baby.
6. A. What are you doing?
   B. I'm listening to music.
7. A. What are you doing?
   B. I'm making dinner.
8. A. What are you doing?
   B. I'm eating lunch.

PAGE 38

Listen and circle the correct words.

1. I study.
2. I'm eating dinner.
3. I exercise.
4. I'm combing my hair.
5. I'm listening to music.
6. I go to work.
7. I read.
8. I'm making lunch.

PAGE 41

Listen and write the number under the correct picture.

1. A. What's the weather?
   B. It's cold.
2. A. What's the weather?
   B. It's cloudy.
3. A. What's the weather?
   B. It's snowing.
4. A. What's the weather?
   B. It's foggy.
5. A. What's the weather?
   B. It's hot.

PAGE 49

Circle the number you hear.

1. There are eight people in the room.
2. There are twenty books on the bookshelf.
3. There are thirteen students in the class.
4. There are forty desks in the classroom.
5. My address is sixteen Pond Road.
6. There are seven people in my family.
7. There are fifty classrooms in the school.
8. The temperature is ninety degrees.

PAGE 49

Write the number you hear.

1. My address is fourteen Main Street.
2. My address is seventy Pond Street.
3. My address is twenty-nine Center Street.
4. My address is thirty-four eleven Central Avenue.
5. My address is eighteen thirty-six Washington Street.
6. My apartment number is two thirty-four.

7. My apartment number is three nineteen.
8. My apartment number is four oh eight.
9. My English class is in Room one twenty-three.
10. My English class is in Room two thirteen.
11. My address is fifteen oh nine Main Street.
12. My address is thirty-two oh seven Central Avenue.

PAGE 51

Circle the time you hear.

1. A. What time is it?
   B. It's eight o'clock.
2. A. What time is it?
   B. It's nine o'clock.
3. A. What time is it?
   B. It's eleven o'clock.
4. A. What time is it?
   B. It's ten thirty.
5. A. What time is it?
   B. It's four o'clock.
6. A. What time is it?
   B. It's two thirty.
7. A. What time is it?
   B. It's three fifteen.
8. A. What time is it?
   B. It's five forty-five.

PAGE 53

Circle the day you hear.

1. I clean my apartment on Friday.
2. I do the laundry on Monday.
3. I play basketball on Saturday.
4. I go to school on Tuesday.
5. My daughter plays the guitar on Sunday.
6. My son washes the dishes on Wednesday.
7. We watch TV on Friday.
8. My grandmother cooks dinner on Thursday.

PAGE 53

Write the time you hear on the correct day.

1. A. Can you come in on Wednesday at three o'clock?
   B. On Wednesday at three o'clock? Yes, I can.
2. A. Can you come in on Friday at ten o'clock?
   B. On Friday at ten o'clock? Yes, I can.
3. A. Can you come in on Monday at nine thirty?
   B. On Monday at nine thirty? Yes, I can.
4. A. Can you come in on Thursday at two fifteen?
   B. On Thursday at two fifteen? Yes, I can.
5. A. Can you come in on Tuesday at one forty-five?
   B. On Tuesday at one forty-five? Yes, I can.

6. A. Can you play basketball on Saturday at eleven thirty?
   B. On Saturday at eleven thirty? Yes, I can.
7. A. Can you come for dinner on Sunday at six o'clock?
   B. On Sunday at six o'clock? Yes, I can. Thank you.

PAGE 55

Circle the number you hear.

1. A. What floor do you live on?
   B. I live on the seventeenth floor.
   A. The seventeenth floor?
   B. Yes. That's right.
2. A. What floor do you live on?
   B. I live on the second floor.
   A. The second floor?
   B. Yes. That's right.
3. A. What floor do you live on?
   B. I'm on the thirteenth floor.
   A. The thirteenth floor?
   B. Yes. That's right.
4. A. Where is your apartment?
   B. It's on the fifteenth floor.
   A. The fifteenth floor?
   B. Yes. That's correct.
5. A. I live on the twelfth floor.
   B. The twelfth floor?
   A. Yes.
6. A. Where is the English classroom?
   B. It's on the third floor.
   A. The third floor?
   B. Yes.
7. A. Is this the twenty-first floor?
   B. Yes. It's the twenty-first floor.
   A. Thank you.
8. A. Is this the fortieth floor?
   B. Yes. It's the fortieth floor.
   A. Thank you.
9. A. Do you live on fifty-seventh Street?
   B. Yes. My apartment is on fifty-seventh Street.
10. A. Does your sister live on ninety-seventh Street?
    B. Yes. Her apartment is on ninety-seventh Street.
11. A. Excuse me. Is this thirty-fifth Street?
    B. Yes. This is thirty-fifth Street.
12. A. Excuse me. Is this nineteenth Street?
    B. Yes. This is nineteenth Street.

PAGE 57

Circle the date you hear.

1. A. What's today's date?
   B. It's April sixteenth.
   A. April sixteenth?
   B. Yes. That's right.
2. A. What's today's date?
   B. It's November twelfth.
   A. November twelfth?
   B. Yes. That's right.
3. A. What's today's date?
   B. It's September third.

A. September third?
   B. Yes. That's correct.
4. A. When is your birthday?
   B. My birthday is June seventh.
   A. June seventh?
   B. Yes.
5. A. When is your birthday?
   B. My birthday is August twenty-first.
   A. August twenty-first?
   B. Yes.
6. A. What's today's date?
   B. It's March second.
   A. March second?
   B. Yes.
7. A. What's the date today?
   B. Today is July tenth.
   A. July tenth?
   B. Yes.
8. A. When is your birthday?
   B. My birthday is October thirty-first.
   A. October thirty-first?
   B. Yes.
9. A. Is your birthday November first?
   B. Yes. It's November first.
10. A. Is today January twentieth?
    B. Yes. It's January twentieth.

PAGE 59

Listen and write the number under the correct picture.

1. A. I just found two dollars and twenty-five cents!
   B. Two dollars and twenty-five cents?
   A. Yes.
2. A. I just found a five-dollar bill!
   B. Five dollars?
   A. Yes.
3. A. I just found a fifty-dollar bill!
   B. Fifty dollars?
   A. Yes.
4. A. Do you have any money?
   B. Yes. I have a dollar bill and ten cents.
   A. A dollar and ten cents?
   B. Yes.
5. A. Do you have any change?
   B. I have fifty-two cents.
   A. Fifty-two cents?
   B. Yes.
6. A. I just found thirty-five dollars!
   B. Thirty-five dollars?
   A. Yes.

PAGE 59

Circle the amount you hear.

1. five cents
2. twenty dollars
3. fifty cents
4. one dollar
5. thirty-five dollars
6. ten cents
7. seventy-five cents
8. one hundred dollars

Listen and write the number under the correct picture.

1. A. Tell me about the apartment.
   B. It has a very nice bathroom
2. A. Please tell me about the apartment.
   B. It has a very nice living room.
3. A. Tell me about the apartment.
   B. It has a very large kitchen.
4. A. Is there a dining room in the apartment?
   B. Yes, there is.
5. A. Please tell me about the bedroom.
   B. It's very large.

PAGE 69

Listen and write the number under the correct picture.

1. A. Is there a shower in the bathroom?
   B. Yes, there is.
2. A. Is there a stove in the kitchen?
   B. Yes, there is.
3. A. Is there a closet in the bedroom?
   B. Yes, there is.
4. A. Is there a fireplace in the living room?
   B. Yes, there is.
5. A. Is there a window in the dining room?
   B. Yes, there is.

PAGE 79

Listen and write the number under the correct picture.

1. A. Where are you going?
   B. I'm going to the library.
2. A. Where are you going?
   B. I'm going to the bus station.
3. A. Where are you going?
   B. I'm going to the laundromat.
4. A. Where are you going?
   B. I'm going to the gas station.
5. A. Where are you going?
   B. I'm going to the bank.

PAGE 81

Listen and write the number under the correct picture.

1. A. Excuse me. Where's the train station?
   B. It's on Central Avenue.
   A. Thanks.
2. A. Excuse me. Where's the movie theater?
   B. It's on Main Street.
   A. Thanks.
3. A. Excuse me. Where's the park?
   B. It's on Lake Street.
   A. Thank you.

4. A. Excuse me. Where's the post office?
   B. It's on Walker Avenue.
   A. Thanks.
5. A. Excuse me. Where's the hospital?
   B. It's on River Road.
   A. Thanks.

PAGE 93

Listen and write the number next to the correct picture.

1. A. What does he look like?
   B. He's short, with gray hair.
2. A. What does she look like?
   B. She's short, with black hair.
3. A. What does she look like?
   B. She's tall, with blond hair.
4. A. What does he look like?
   B. He's average height, with brown hair.
5. A. What does she look like?
   B. She's average height, with brown hair.

PAGE 105

Listen and write the number under the correct picture.

1. I'm looking for an apple.
2. I'm looking for apples.
3. There aren't any more oranges.
4. I'm looking for a banana.
5. I'm looking for an orange.
6. There aren't any more bananas.

PAGE 107

Listen and write the number under the correct picture.

1. There isn't any more cheese.
2. I'm looking for milk.
3. There isn't any more soda.
4. I'm looking for sugar.
5. There isn't any more lettuce.
6. I'm looking for bread.

PAGE 111

Listen and write the number under the correct picture.

1. We need a jar of mayonnaise.
2. We need a bag of sugar.
3. We need a box of cookies.
4. I'm looking for a loaf of bread.
5. I'm looking for a can of soup.
6. We need a bunch of bananas.
7. We need a pound of cheese.
8. I'm looking for a dozen eggs.

PAGE 113

Listen and write the number under the correct picture.

1. A. Can I help you?
   B. Yes. I'd like a hot dog, please.
2. A. Can I help you?
   B. Yes. I'd like a pizza, please.
3. A. May I help you?
   B. Yes. I'd like a taco, please.
4. A. May I help you?
   B. Yes, please. I'd like a sandwich.

5. A. Can I help you?
   B. Yes. I'd like lemonade, please.

PAGE 121

Listen and write the number under the correct picture.

1. A. I'm looking for a coat.
   B. Coats are over there.
   A. Thank you.
2. A. I'm looking for a blouse.
   B. Blouses are over there.
   A. Thank you.
3. A. I'm looking for a shirt.
   B. Shirts are over there.
   A. Thank you.
4. A. May I help you?
   B. Yes. I'm looking for a suit.
   A. Suits are over there.
   B. Thank you.
5. A. May I help you?
   B. Yes. I'm looking for a dress.
   A. Dresses are over there.
   B. Thanks.

PAGE 123

Listen and write the number under the correct picture.

1. A. May I help you?
   B. Yes. I'm looking for a pair of pajamas.
2. A. May I help you?
   B. Yes. I'm looking for a pair of jeans.
3. A. May I help you?
   B. Yes. I'm looking for a pair of shoes.
4. A. May I help you?
   B. Yes. I'm looking for a pair of gloves.
5. A. May I help you?
   B. Yes. I'm looking for a pair of mittens.
6. A. May I help you?
   B. Yes, please. I'm looking for a pair of socks.
7. A. I'm looking for a suit.
   B. Suits are over there.
8. A. I'm looking for a pair of pants.
   B. Pants are over there.

PAGE 135

Listen and write the number under the correct picture.

1. A. Where's the deposit slip?
   B. The deposit slip? Here it is.
2. A. Where's my ATM card?
   B. Your ATM card? Here it is.
3. A. Where's the check?
   B. The check is on the table.
4. A. Where's the withdrawal slip?
   B. The withdrawal slip? Here it is.
5. A. I'm looking for the checkbook.
   B. The checkbook is in the living room.
6. A. I'm looking for my credit card.
   B. I think your credit card is in the kitchen.

PAGE 147

Listen and write the number under the correct picture.

1. She has a headache.
2. He has a cold.
3. I have a backache.
4. He has a toothache.
5. She has a cough.

PAGE 149

Listen and write the number next to the correct medicine.

1. I have a cough. What should I use?
2. I have an earache. What should I use?
3. I have a stomachache. What should I use?
4. I have a sore throat. What should I use?
5. I have a headache. What should I use?

PAGE 151

Listen and write the number under the correct picture.

1. A. What's the problem?
   B. I have an earache.
2. A. What's the problem?
   B. My back hurts.
3. A. What's the matter?
   B. My neck hurts.
4. A. What's the problem?
   B. I have a stomachache.
5. A. What's the matter?
   B. My arm hurts.

PAGE 163

Listen and write the number under the correct picture.

1. My favorite subject is music.
2. My favorite subject is social studies.
3. My favorite subject is math.
4. My favorite subject is science.
5. My favorite subject is English.
6. My favorite subject is technology.

PAGE 165

Listen and write the number under the correct picture.

1. I have orchestra practice after school today.
2. I play basketball with my friends after school.
3. My daughter is in the band at her school.
4. We have soccer practice every afternoon.
5. The choir is practicing in the music room.
6. My son practices football every day after school.

PAGE 173

Listen and write the number under the correct Help Wanted sign.

1. A. What kind of job are you looking for?
   B. I'm looking for a job as a cashier.

2. A. What kind of job are you looking for?
   B. I'm looking for a job as a delivery person.
3. A. What kind of job do you want?
   B. I'm looking for a job as a cook.
4. A. What kind of job are you looking for?
   B. I'm looking for a job as a gardener.
5. A. What kind of work are you looking for?
   B. I'm looking for a job as a construction worker.
6. A. What kind of work do you want to do?
   B. I want to work as a custodian.

PAGE 175

Listen and write the number under the correct want ad.

1. I can drive a taxi.
2. I can bake.
3. I can type.
4. I can fix cars.
5. I can paint.

PAGE 191

Look at the map above. Listen and circle the correct place.

1. It's on the left.
2. It's on the right.
3. It's across from the laundromat.
4. It's next to the bus station.
5. It's on the right, across from the hospital.
6. It's on the left, across from the train station.
7. It's on the right, next to the park.
8. It's on the left, between the library and the hospital.

PAGE 193

Listen and write the number under the correct picture.

1. A. Excuse me. How do I get to the mall?
   B. Take Bus Number 11.
   A. Bus Number 11? Thank you.
2. A. Excuse me. How do I get to City Hall?
   B. Take the E Train.
   A. The E Train? Thanks.
3. A. Excuse me. How do I get to the Midtown Hospital?
   B. Take the C Train.
   A. The C Train?
   B. Yes.
   A. Thank you.
4. A. Excuse me. How do I get to the airport?
   B. Take the Blue Line.
   A. The Blue Line? Thanks.
5. A. Excuse me. How do I get to the library?
   B. Take Bus Number 23.
   A. Number 23? Thanks.

PAGE 195

Listen and write the number under the correct sign.

1. A. Excuse me. Where do I get off for City Hall?
   B. Get off at K Street.
   A. K Street? Thank you.
2. A. Excuse me. Where do I get off for the West Town Mall?
   B. Get off at 11th Avenue.
   A. 11th Avenue? Thanks.
3. A. Excuse me. Where do I get off for Jefferson Memorial Hospital?
   B. Get off at 7th Avenue.
   A. 7th Avenue? Thank you.
4. A. Excuse me. Where do I get off for the central library?
   B. Get off at J Street.
   A. J Street? Thanks.
5. A. Excuse me. Where do I get off for Miller's Department Store?
   B. Get off at 2nd Avenue.
   A. 2nd Avenue? Thanks.

PAGE 205

Listen and write the number under the correct picture.

1. I like to go swimming.
2. I like to play tennis.
3. I like to go dancing.
4. I like to play soccer.
5. I like to go jogging.

PAGE 207

Listen and write the number under the correct picture.

1. A. What are you going to do tomorrow?
   B. I'm going to go to the park.
2. A. What are you going to do tomorrow?
   B. I'm going to see a movie.
3. A. What are you going to do tomorrow?
   B. I'm going to play baseball.
4. A. What are you going to do tomorrow?
   B. I'm going to see a play.
5. A. What are you going to do tomorrow?
   B. I'm going to go to the zoo.

PAGE 209

Listen and circle the correct word.

1. I went to the zoo yesterday.
2. I like to listen to music.
3. I exercised yesterday morning.
4. I exercise every day.
5. I like to go dancing.
6. I played soccer this morning.
7. I went to the park.
8. I saw a movie.

The numbers next to each topic indicate the pages on which the words first appear—usually in the Vocabulary Preview section at the beginning of each unit.

Ailments 145

backache
cold
cough
earache
fever
headache
sore throat
stomachache
toothache

Bank 132

ATM card
bank
bank book
check
checkbook
credit card
deposit slip
withdrawal slip

Body 144

arm
back
ear
eye
finger
foot
hand
head
leg
neck
nose
stomach

Classroom Actions 26–27

Close your book.
Erase your name.
Go to the board.
Open your book.
Point to the clock.
Put away your book.
Raise your hand.
Sit down.
Stand up.
Take out your book.
Write your name.

Classroom Objects & People 18–19

board
book
bookshelf
bulletin board
calculator
chair
chalk
clock
computer
desk
eraser
globe
map
notebook
overhead projector
pen
pencil
ruler
screen
student
table
teacher
TV
wall

Clothing 118–119

belt
blouse
coat
dress
gloves
jacket
jeans
mittens
necklace
pajamas
pants
shirt
shoes
skirt
socks
suit
sweater
tie
umbrella
watch

Clothing Sizes 119

small
medium
large
extra-large

Colors 124

black
blue
brown
gray
green
orange
pink
purple
red
white
yellow

Days of the Week 47

Sunday
Monday
Tuesday
Wednesday
Thursday
Friday
Saturday

Describing Feelings 95

afraid
angry
happy
hungry
sad
sick
thirsty
tired

Describing People 88–89, 98

age
  young
  middle-aged
  old

height
  tall
  average height
  short

weight
  heavy
  average weight
  thin

marital status
  single
  married
  divorced
  widowed

hair
  black
  blond
  brown
  gray
  red
  white

eyes
  blue
  green
  brown

Everyday Activities 32–33

brush my teeth
clean
comb my hair
come home
cook dinner
do the laundry
eat breakfast
eat dinner
eat lunch
exercise
feed the baby
get dressed
get undressed
get up
go to bed
go to school
go to work
iron
listen to music
make breakfast
make dinner
make lunch
play basketball
play the guitar
read
study
take a shower
walk the dog
wash the dishes
watch TV

Family Members 12–13

aunt
brother
cousin
daughter
father
granddaughter
grandfather
grandmother
grandson
husband
mother
nephew
niece
sister
son
uncle
wife

Food 102–103

apple
banana
bread
butter
carrot
cereal
cheese
cheeseburger
coffee
cookie
donut
egg
hamburger
hot dog
ice cream
lemonade
lettuce
mayonnaise
milk
onion
orange
peach
pizza
potato
sandwich
soda
soup
sugar
taco
tea
tomato

Food Containers & Quantities 110

bag
bottle
box
bunch
can
dozen
jar
loaf
pound
quart

Home 64–65, 71

apartment
apartment building
balcony
bathroom
bathtub
bed
bedroom
cabinet
chair
closet
dining room
dormitory
duplex
fireplace
house
kitchen
lamp
living room
mobile home
patio
refrigerator
rug
shelter
shower
sofa
stove
table
window

Injuries 151

broke my arm
broke my leg
burned my hand
cut my face
cut my finger
sprained my wrist

Job Skills 174, 178

assemble
bake
cook
cut
drive
fix
operate
paint
repair
sell
teach
type
use

Location 189

across from
between
next to
on the left
on the right

Medicine 148, 152, 154

antacid tablets
aspirin
caplet
capsule
cold medicine
cough syrup
ear drops
pill
tablespoon
tablet
teaspoon
throat lozenges
vitamin

Money 47

dime
dollar bill
half dollar
nickel
penny
quarter

Months of the Year 47

January
February
March
April
May
June
July
August
September
October
November
December

SKILL INDEX

BASIC LANGUAGE SKILLS

Alphabet, 2, 5, 6–7

Listening, 6, 9, 11, 23, 27, 35, 37, 38, 41, 49, 51, 53, 55, 57, 59, 67, 69, 79, 81, 93, 105, 107, 111, 113, 121, 123, 135, 147, 149, 151, 163, 165, 173, 175, 191, 193, 195, 205, 207, 209

Speaking
(*Throughout*)

Reading/Document literacy
Abbreviations:
    Days of the week, 53
    Food quantities, 114
    Months of the year, 57
    States, 11
Calendar, 47, 52–53, 56–57, 210, 211–212
Cash register display, 140
Checks, 136
Cloze reading, 79, 81, 91, 153, 184
Destination signs on public transportation, 192–193
Diagram, 13, 149, 181
Envelope, 139
Form, 11, 15–16, 99–100, 177
Help Wanted signs, 173
List, 29–30, 43–44, 115–116, 185–186
Map, 41, 85–86, 189, 190–191
Medicine labels, 154
Menu, 141–142
Narrative paragraph, 72, 198, 210
Newspaper, finding information in, 41
Paycheck, 184
Safety signs, 183
Schedules:
    Bus schedule, 198, 199–200
    Class schedule, 166, 167–168
    Train schedule, 61–62
    Work schedule, 184
Store directory, 129–130, 155–156
Street signs, 194
Traffic signs, 189, 196–197
Want ads, 175, 177

Writing
Addresses, 11, 84
Charts, writing information in, 7, 83, 91, 95, 113, 127, 135, 151, 153, 163, 165, 179, 195, 205, 207
Check, 137
Cloze reading, 79, 81, 91, 153, 184
Days of the week, 53, 60
Forms, filling out, 11, 97, 177

Journal writing, 14, 28, 42, 60, 72, 84, 98, 114, 128, 140, 154, 166, 184, 198, 210
Name, 5, 7
Schedule, 139
Shopping list, 114
Signs, 181, 183, 197
Telephone number, 8–9
Time, 51, 60, 61–62, 139, 198, 199–200

NUMBERS/NUMERACY/MATH

Addition, 48
Address numbers, 10–11
Age, 14, 42, 98
Cardinal numbers, 2, 8–9, 10–11, 28, 42, 46, 48–49, 72, 166, 210
Counting items to take inventory, 28
Dates, 57, 210
Destination signs on public transportation, 192–193
Dosages on medicine labels, 154
Height, 98
Money, amounts of, 58–59, 136–137, 140, 184
Ordinal numbers, 54–55, 72, 84, 129–130, 166, 210
Prices, 128
Pronouncing similar numbers, 49
Route numbers on public transportation, 192–193, 195
Saying large address numbers, 49
Saying room numbers, 49, 166
Schedule information, 198
Subtraction, 140
Telephone numbers, 8–9
Temperatures, 42
Time, 50–51, 167–168, 184, 198, 199–200, 211–212
Weight, 98

LEARNING SKILLS

Categorization, 109
Chronological order, 35
Diagrams, 13, 14, 149, 181

GRAMMAR (Integrated)

Adjectives, 88–95, 125, 127
Agent nouns, 174–175
Articles: A/An, 24–25
Can, 52, 112, 138, 149, 150, 155–156, 174–175, 178–179, 185–186
Count/Non-count nouns, 106–107
Future: Going to, 164, 206–207, 211–212
Have/Has, 66–67, 92, 146–147, 148–149, 164
Imperatives, 26–27, 70, 93, 114, 149, 154, 155–156, 182–183, 190, 192–193, 194, 196
Like to, 204–205, 209
May, 122
Partitives, 110–111, 114

GRAMMAR (Explicit Mini-Lessons)

APPLICATIONS

LEARNING STRATEGIES